How To Keep The Creditors From Coming To Your Home

Randy Morrison

A common-sense approach to life

How to Keep the Creditors from Coming to Your Home
A Common Sense Approach

Common Sense Approach
515 Jersey Avenue
Golden Valley, MN 55426
www.commonsenseapproach.org

Unless otherwise indicated, all Scripture quotations are from the New King James Version.

ISBN 0-944129-05-6
Printed in the United States of America.

Dedication

I dedicate this book first and foremost to my mother for bringing me into this world and for giving me the chance to become all that God intended for me to be. Although it was hard for her to raise a child by herself with few resources, she made do with what she had. She never lived beyond her means. I will never forget what she taught me about money. She said, "Never buy what you can't pay for." That advice has stuck with me all my life. So, thank you, Mom, for your common sense and also for being a good example when it comes to financial responsibility. I love you.

I also dedicate this book to all those desiring a common-sense way out of financial challenges. Decisions made today about finances will impact the lives of the next generation. My heart's desire is for us to leave a legacy for this generation, built on practical, common-sense steps and principles for a productive and rewarding life. The steps taken today toward living a life of financial freedom will have long-lasting results for the next generation.

Contents

Acknowledgements

I give thanks to God for the wisdom to put this book together. The passion to help others live life by design and not from crisis to crisis in financial areas has burned within my heart for years. Bringing this book to reality—so others can benefit—has been my heart's desire.

I want to acknowledge Lindsay Willis for the countless hours, commitment, and effort she made to assist me throughout this writing process. I could not have done it without her input. Lindsay, you are a God-send.

I also acknowledge the expertise and encouragement of Dr. Heather Huseby-Dawson for helping me turn the vision of this book into a reality.

I especially thank the staff of Speak the Word Church International for their dedicated support. It is with special appreciation that I acknowledge the continuous support received from the entire Speak the Word Church International family. Their continuing love and encouragement is a true blessing in light of all we have been through together. Thank you for sticking with me and allowing me the opportunity to minister into your lives. You are the best.

Preface

The Story

2 Kings 4:1-7

“[1]A certain woman of the wives of the sons of the prophets cried out to Elisha, saying, ‘Your servant my husband is dead, and you know that your servant feared the Lord. And the creditor is coming to take my two sons to be his slaves.’

[2]So Elisha said to her, ‘What shall I do for you? Tell me, what do you have in the house?’ And she said, ‘Your maidservant has nothing in the house but a jar of oil.’

[3]Then he said, ‘Go, borrow vessels from everywhere, from all your neighbors—empty vessels; do not gather just a few. [4]And when you have come in, you shall shut the door behind you and your sons; then pour it into all those vessels, and set aside the full ones.’

[5]So she went from him and shut the door behind her and her sons, who brought the vessels to her; and she poured it out. [6]Now it came to pass, when the vessels were full, that she said to her son, ‘Bring me another vessel.’

And he said to her, ‘There is not another vessel.’ So the oil ceased. [7]Then she came and told the man of God. And he said, ‘Go, sell the oil and pay your debt; and you and your sons live on the rest.’”

GOD WORKED
TO GET WHAT
HE *WANTED*;
HE EXPECTS
US TO WORK
TO GET WHAT
***WE WANT* OUT**
OF THIS LIFE.

Introduction

My desire in writing this book is to help people live their lives responsibly when it comes to finances. I want to challenge some of the so-called religious thinking that people have in the area of finances.

Many people look for a *quick and easy* way to change their financial condition, without understanding that their own thinking put them into a poor financial situation in the first place. I want to *change your thinking,* so you can *change your financial condition*. Maybe you have heard the saying, "If you keep doing what you've always done, you will keep receiving what you've always gotten." It's true—especially in the area of finances. Too many people keep making the same mistakes over and over and over again. And each time, they hope it turns out differently. But it never does, because they never change the way they think. If we are willing to change our way of thinking, we can change our results.

Why write another book about finances? Because you need money. I need it. We all need money to function in society today. But, many in the Body of Christ are not good at managing money when they get it. If all Christians were good at managing money, the world would be running to us for answers to their financial problems. We would be loaning money *to* the world rather than borrowing money *from* the world, just to make next month's rent payment.

THE BIBLE IS GOD'S INSTRUCTION BOOK FOR LIFE

Many in the church are in financial trouble. They need to learn how to handle their finances in order to keep the creditors from coming to their home. I want to provide some common-sense principles to help. Not the kind of help, though, that is full of hype with no substance. I want to help people improve their financial conditions on a lasting basis. I don't want people to simply endure poor financial circumstances, when they have the power to change these circumstances themselves.

I believe the Bible is God's instruction book for life. In it we find information needed to be successful in life. This includes learning how to be successful in our financial lives. The Bible tells us clearly how we should manage our finances. I believe if we follow what the Bible says, we can prosper and be a blessing to a lost and dying world. I believe if we follow the instructions the Bible gives us, we can avoid financial crises in life.

You may be asking, "Where do I find that in the Bible, Brother Randy?" Look with me at Joshua 1:8 in the Amplified Bible. It states: *"This Book of the Law shall not depart out of your mouth, but you shall* ***meditate*** *on it day and night, that you may* ***observe and do*** *according to all that is written in it. For* ***then you shall make your way prosperous,*** *and then you shall* ***deal wisely*** *and* ***have good success.****"*

Notice the end of this verse first. It states: we can *make our way prosperous;* we can *deal wisely;* and we can *have good suc-*

cess. These phrases don't need much explanation. They simply say we can be successful in life.

Now, we could probably debate all day long on the meaning of success in life. But, rather than arguing about what success is, can we agree on one simple thing? I think we can agree that **failing financially** in life is **not** dealing wisely. It is not having good success; it is not making our way prosperous.

I am writing this book so people can keep the creditors from coming to their home. I am writing this book so people can deal wisely and have good *financial* success in life. I am writing this book so that Christians will no longer fail financially in life.

You see, success starts with our mindset. Success is not just the amount of money we make. It is the way we think about life. There were times in my life when I did not have a lot of money. But, I had a success mentality, and that mentality helped me change my circumstances in life. I want to help you develop that kind of thinking.

A COMMON-SENSE APPROACH TO LIFE

I take a common-sense approach to finances. One of the foundational Scriptures I want you to keep in mind as you read this book is Proverbs 24:3 from The Living Bible. It states: *"Any enterprise is built by wise planning, becomes strong through common sense, and profits wonderfully by keeping abreast of the facts."* Now, this is information that can change a life. Let's look at this in more depth.

You may ask, "What is an enterprise?" Good question. You might first think this refers to the Star Trek spaceship, *Enterprise.*

Well, let me assure you that Proverbs 24:3 is *not* talking about *that* Enterprise.

An "enterprise" is any endeavor we attempt in life. It could mean marriage, family, business, or career. More specifically, an "enterprise" can be your church ministry, writing a book, building a home, or planning for retirement. In the context of this book, I consider "enterprise" to be those factors necessary to build a successful life, specifically in the financial realm.

Look at what it takes to be successful in building an enterprise: *wise planning, common sense,* and *keeping abreast of the facts.* I suggest these three factors are really lacking in many of our lives today.

Life is lived at such a rapid pace that we just don't take the time to plan. Common sense has become so uncommon that it is no longer common sense, and there never seems to be enough time to keep on top of all the information coming at us. I want to emphasize the value of common sense when it comes to finances. I want to make common sense common again! I fully believe when we live our financial lives with a common-sense approach, we will never have the creditors coming to our home.

COMMON SENSE PUTS AN END TO THE "MIRAGE" OF WEALTH

Unfortunately, many people live in such a spiritual mirage about their finances that they often cannot tell the difference between reality and illusion. Too many people get consumed looking for an escape from reality. Just when they think they have found it, they become disappointed, because there really is *no* escape from reality.

I think some of the teaching in the Body of Christ has fueled a mirage mentality when it comes to wealth. I simply don't agree with it; I want to bring us back to reality.

You and I have heard preachers talk about "Debt Cancellation," "How to Pay Your Bills Supernaturally," or "Supernatural Debt Reduction." It all sounds good, doesn't it? Sounds real spiritual, right? But, does the Bible really promise us these things? Can we really expect God to do things like this for us? I don't think so. It is what I call the "mirage mentality," and I want to challenge that thinking.

Let me be blunt with you: ***there is no supernatural way out of debt!*** Read the following Scripture (Proverbs 28:20) from THE MESSAGE Bible: *"Committed and persistent work pays off; get-rich-quick schemes are rip-offs."* This Scripture makes it very clear, doesn't it? Money has to be earned. Bills have to be paid. Expenses have to be managed. Money must be saved. It takes work...*hard* work and discipline. The Bible does not provide any get-rich-quick schemes to bail us out of financial difficulties. God wants us to be responsible when it comes to finances. God wants us to work in order to prosper. And then we must wisely manage the money we earn.

Everything you see in this physical world is a result of someone working to bring it about.

Some people in the Body of Christ don't like to hear anything about working to be successful. But, one of the conditions for being blessed is that we must work. We don't get to sit around, be idle and then expect God's blessings.

Everything that exists took *effort* to make it happen. That is the pattern God gave us in the beginning. Read Genesis 2:1-3. It states:

> *"[1]Thus the heavens and the earth, and all the host of them, were finished. [2]And on the seventh day God ended* ***His work*** *which* ***He had done****, and He rested on the seventh day from all* ***His work*** *which* ***He had done****. [3]Then God blessed the seventh day and sanctified it, because in it He rested from all* ***His work*** *which God had created and made."*

Now, think with me for a moment. If **God** had to work to get what **He** wanted, what makes **us** think that we do **not** have to work to get what **we** want? You see, friends, I believe the reason so many people don't like to work is because they don't understand what work is; work is *not* necessarily manual labor.

I think it's helpful to differentiate between "having a job" and "going to work." The "having a job" mentality is simply having an occupation, something that *occupies* your time. It *employs* you. It makes you busy, but it does not make you effective. It is only the maintenance of a task. It is doing the minimum to get by. The "having a job" mentality is limited; it's a dead end.

The "going to work" mentality achieves an objective. It is focused on a result you want. It is the transference of energy, the exercising of one's skill, and the release of creativity. The "going to work" mentality *deploys* you—it *puts you and your creative ability into action*. It is where you get your inspiration; it allows you to use your knowledge. "Going to work" means you are taking steps to do something you love; you enjoy doing it.

God loved to work. He worked six days before He rested. I believe work is where you will find true satisfaction and fulfillment here on this human planet. And, it is one part of keeping the creditors from coming to our home.

There is a different mentality between "having a job" and "going to work." Work is releasing the creative energy within us to bring to pass the things we love.

A COMMON SENSE APPROACH TO LIFE

I believe in order to succeed in life we need a common-sense approach to life. I told you that common sense was going to be a theme in this book, and now I'm talking about it again. Many of the things I will share in this book will go against some of the religious ideas that have been taught in churches or on television. It will go against the "mirage mentality" of wealth that has developed in some people's thinking.

Why am I doing this? I have seen too many well-meaning Christians buy into the lie of the "mirage mentality," the lie of "financial miracles," or the lie of "supernatural debt reduction." They are told by preachers that all they have to do is give, and God will work a "financial miracle" for them. Or, they are told to pray and God will "supernaturally" put money in their bank accounts.

This can "preach good" in the pulpit to ignorant, nonproductive, and irresponsible people, but in realty, *none of it is true!*

If we could just *"give our way out of debt,"* why are those preachers who are promoting these myths relying on *your* giving for their ministry to survive? If all we need to do is pray and God will give us money, why are these preachers receiving offerings in their meetings?

The financial breakthrough for these preachers comes from your offerings to them. Have you ever thought about this? If financial breakthroughs come by giving, why aren't they giving to the people they are teaching? Why are they always the ones receiving, and the people are always the ones giving?

I am not mad at any preacher. I just want to teach you the truth. I will not lie to you just so you feel good and get all excited about something that simply isn't true.

As you read this book, I pray you will develop a commonsense approach to managing money— to keep the creditors from coming to your home. I believe as you read this book, the following three things will happen to you:

- You will be inspired!
- You will be challenged!
- Your thinking about work and money will be transformed!

When your thinking is transformed, your life will change! Let the truths I share in this book bring true financial freedom to your life!

COMMON SENSE IDEAS

1. The Bible is God's instruction book on life.

2. There is no supernatural way to get out of debt.

3. Everything around us is a result of someone working to bring it about.

4. God worked to get what He wanted; He expects us to work to get what we want.

5. Jobs employ; work deploys.

6. Work releases creative energy from within to bring to pass things loved.

7. Too many people live in a mirage of wealth.

NEW ACTION MUST BE TAKEN TO CHANGE A **SITUATION. DOING THE SAME OLD THING WILL NOT CHANGE A** ***FINANCIAL SITUATION.***

Chapter 1

The Answer Is in the Problem!

2 Kings 4:1-7

*“[1]A certain woman of the wives of the sons of the prophets cried out to Elisha, saying, ‘***Your servant, my husband*** is dead, and you know that your servant feared the LORD. And* **the creditor is coming** *to take my two sons to be his slaves.’*

[2]So Elisha said to her, ‘What shall I do for you? Tell me, **what do you have in the house?**’ *And she said, ‘***Your maidservant has nothing*** in the house but* **a jar of oil.**’

*[3]Then he said, ‘***Go, borrow vessels*** from everywhere, from all your neighbors—empty vessels; do not gather just a few. [4]And when you have come in, you shall shut the door behind you and your sons; then pour it into all those vessels, and* **set aside the full ones.**’

[5]So she went from him and shut the door behind her and her sons, who brought the vessels to her; and she poured it out. [6]Now it came to pass, when the vessels were full, that she said to her son, ‘Bring me another vessel.’

*And he said to her, ‘There is not another vessel.’ So the oil ceased. [7]Then she came and told the man of God. And he said, ‘***Go, sell the oil and pay your debt****; and you and your sons* **live on the rest**.’”

I have heard a lot of sermons based on this passage of Scripture in the past few years. Many of these sermons teach that this is a story about "supernatural debt reduction" or a "financial miracle." I will use this story as the basis for this book, which presents a common-sense approach to finances. I believe the teachings on "supernatural debt reduction" and "financial miracles" are missing some very important principles hidden in this story. Because people are not being taught the principles from this story, they believe lies about their finances. I want us to *really* find out what happens in this story, rather than just believe the hype that some people preach. Take a closer look at this story with me, will you?

A WIDOW WOMAN WITH BAD DEBT

This is the story of a widow woman. Her husband was a man of God, and he died. He left his wife and their sons without any source of income and deeply in debt. They had so much debt that the creditors were coming to their home to take her sons in order to pay the debt. Now that is what I call bad debt! She could not pay the debt, so she ran to the man of God. His name was Elisha. Notice how she referred to her husband when she talked to Elisha. She called him *"your servant, my husband."* To me, that means Elisha knew this man pretty well. This man and his family were no strangers to Elisha. I believe she came to Elisha because Elisha knew the family and knew that the man of God had given his life for God.

But there is something here I don't understand. I don't understand why she thought her financial problems were Elisha's responsibility. Why does serving in the house of God make people think they are entitled to make it the Church's responsibility to pay off their debts? Such thinking is based on some unscriptural thinking, if you ask me. Yet, many Christians think the Church should be their bank or they think the Church should provide relief from their financial problems.

I don't know if you realize this, but the Church's responsibility is to equip you to live your life with good self-government. The Church does not exist to solve all your problems—especially your financial problems. The purpose of the Church is to teach you principles from God's Word so that *you* can solve *your* problems. The Church does not exist to rescue you from the financial problems you create.

Why do I believe that? Because of the way Elisha responded to this widow woman. What did Elisha, the man of God, say to this woman? Did he take the responsibility for her financial situation? Did he jump up and run out and pay her bills? NO! He asked her a question: "Tell me, what do you have in the home?" Read that question carefully. Elisha did not accept the responsibility for this woman's situation. He made it clear it was her responsibility. He looked at her and asked, "What do *you* have?"

He turned her attention to *her* resources. He made her look at what *she* had, not what *he* had. He made it clear to her that he did not have the resources to solve her problem. She had them herself.

Let's read on. She answered Elisha's question about what she had with one simple word: "NOTHING!!" She said, "Your maidservant has nothing…." From her perspective, she couldn't see anything that could help her out of this situation. *But Elisha could.*

> ***The natural mind sees things, but a spiritual mind looks into things.***

Initially, this widow woman thought she could do nothing about her situation. Then, almost as an afterthought, she added that she did have a jar of oil.

To her that jar of oil did not mean much. She was *looking* at her answer, but she could not *see* it. She looked right at the cruse of oil, but could not see any more than just oil in a jar. But, Elisha knew that cruse of oil was her answer. He just wanted to help her see that she had the answer to her own situation. Elisha saw an opportunity!

Every problem has a solution built into it. God designed it that way. If we can grab onto this thought, it will change our perspective on life forever. *The solution to our problems lies hidden within the problems themselves.*

I believe we have become so used to our surroundings that we sometimes do not recognize what is directly in front of us. We look at things every day, but we really don't see them. For instance, can you answer the following questions?

- What is the color of your neighbor's car?
- How many houses are there on the street where you live?
- What is the color of your child's or your spouse's eyes?

Have trouble answering any of these questions? If you had trouble answering, you are starting to "see" my point, because you probably look at these things *every day!*

Here is another example. When is the last time you looked at the logo on a FedEx truck? Did you know that logo contains more than what you might think? In fact, there is an arrow hidden within the logo. Next time you see a Fed Ex truck passing by, look at it carefully. The arrow is there! You have to *look* for it to *see* it. If you do not see it, look again. Things like this logo are not as they appear at first glance. It takes effort to find what is really there.

THE ANSWER TO THE PROBLEM LIES WITHIN THE PROBLEM

These may be simple things. But I want to emphasize them, because we spend so much of our time seeing problems that we rarely see the solutions to the problems. As long as we settle for only what we can see, we will never discover what we do not see.

2 Corinthians 4:18 states:

> *"18 While we do not look at the things which are seen (or perceived by our physical senses), but at the things which are not seen. For the things which are seen are temporary, but the things which are not seen are eternal."*

We must learn to see that our circumstances are always temporary. That means they are subject to change! But *we* must *do something* to change them. Circumstances do not change on their own. The solution to our problem lies within the problem!

A problem is simply a mismatch between what you are experiencing and what you want out of life.

WHAT WE SEE IS NOT ALL THERE IS

Elisha wanted the woman to change her circumstances. He did not just want to remove her from the problem, because if he did that, he knew it would only be a matter of time before she was back in the same situation.

So what did Elisha do? He gave her a series of instructions that would help change her life forever. He showed her that the answer to her problem was right in front of her, but she had to *do something* to change her circumstances. He saw her answer, and he helped her discover that answer.

First, he told her to go and borrow vessels—as many as she could. Then she was to take them home, close the door behind her, and start using what she had. She was to start pouring the oil. Look at this! The man of God told her *she* had to *do something*. He required her to use what she had, even though she didn't think it was very much.

Have you ever stopped to think how foolish this widow woman must have thought this whole process was? Can you imagine what she was thinking as she went to borrow all those vessels? "This is the most ridiculous thing I have ever done. I cannot believe I am doing this! What good is this going to do? I still don't have anything to solve my problem! I just wanted him to pay my bills, and look what he told me to do! I am running around town borrowing vessels for no reason!"

What we know is the sum total of all that we have learned up to this point in life. Therefore, in order to get something different out of life, we have to acquire new information.

Our breakthroughs always start when we are willing to use what we have.

An instruction from God is always His way of helping us solve our problems. His instructions always lead us to new information. God wants us to learn something new through the process of obeying Him. His instructions are designed to test our obedience. Our obedience to what we hear will position us to receive the blessing of God. Bottom line, God's instructions will bring us new information so that we can change our position in life.

Now back to the widow. After she borrowed all the vessels she could find, she started pouring. The oil started running, and it did not quit until she had run out of vessels. When she had filled all the vessels she had borrowed, she had a room full of oil.

Unfortunately, she still did not see what she *really* had. She still did not *see* the solution, even though she was *looking* right at it. So she went back to the man of God. What did he do? He gave her more instructions—things that *she* had to do. He told her to sell the oil, pay her debts, and live on the rest. *She* had to *sell* the oil. *She* had to *pay* the debts. *She* had to *live on the rest* of the money.

I want you to notice that Elisha did not release her from the responsibility of the debt. There was no "supernatural debt reduction." There were no cancelled debts. She had to *work!* She had to *work* to borrow vessels. She had to *work* to sell the oil. She had to *pay off the debt.* Elisha told her she had to learn how to manage what she had in order to live on the rest.

GOD WANTS US TO USE OUR OPPORTUNITIES RATHER THAN WAIT FOR "FINANCIAL MIRACLES"

Was this a "financial miracle?" No, this was not a *financial* miracle. There *was* a divine intervention, because one small cruse of oil filled many vessels. But that, by itself, is not a *financial* miracle. If we focus only on the oil multiplying, we miss the fact that God empowered this woman to change her circumstances. God did *not* cancel her debts. And God did not just put the money in her bank account. God gave her an opportunity!

I believe God empowered this woman by providing her with an entrepreneurial opportunity. Do you realize opportunity does not *knock* on your door? It stands by silently, waiting to be recognized. Many times opportunity goes unnoticed because it disguises itself in work clothes; we then miss the financial opportunity God has offered. In other words, we look for a miracle instead of looking for an opportunity. We always look for the easy way out. But

To get what we want out of life, we may have to depart from what we have learned in the past.

God has not equipped us with His Spirit and abilities to take the easy way out.

Let me share a truth with you about finances: *the majority of our financial breakthroughs will come as we use our God-given abilities and increase our value. They will not come as a result of some so-called "financial miracle!"*

GOD HAS A PRACTICAL APPROACH TO FINANCES

Why do some preachers tell people to believe in "supernatural debt reduction" or "supernatural debt cancellation?" Is that really what God wants? Should we really believe things like that? Or, does the Bible teach something else?

I believe the Bible is practical. The Bible has a practical approach to everything in our lives, including our finances. And, I believe God wants each of us to live responsibly.

I am trying to get us to think about what we believe and how we live. Why am I emphasizing this? Because, what we believe determines how we live. No *spiritual gimmick* is going to get us out of financial difficulties. We need to use the abilities God has given us, take advantage of the opportunities that come our way, and manage the resources that God brings into our hands.

I believe there are four Common Sense Points we can take from this story in 2 Kings. Each of these following points reveals a practical approach to finances.

1. ***We must be willing to take responsibility for managing our financial lives.***

2. We must become producers in this life rather than living our lives solely as consumers.

3. We must manage the money we make by controlling our expenses.

4. We must learn to save and invest wisely.

Let's take a closer look at each of these four points.

- <u>Common Sense Point 1:</u>
  We must be willing to take responsibility for managing our financial lives.

  Our finances are what they are because of the decisions we have made in life. We cannot blame God or the devil or other people for where we are financially. God never promised "financial miracles" as a way to escape financial difficulties.

- <u>Common Sense Point 2:</u>
  We must become producers in this life rather than living our lives solely as consumers.

  We must learn to use the abilities and opportunities God gives us to earn the money we need in life. We have to change the way we look at life in order to become Producers rather than waste our opportunities and live as Consumers.

- <u>Common Sense Point 3:</u>
  We must manage the money we make by controlling our expenses.

We must discipline our spending to preserve our future. We must learn to manage the seasons in life. We *can* live on less than we think. We must focus on paying off our debts, rather than believing God will cancel them while we remain irresponsible in the management of finances.

- Common Sense Point 4:
  We must learn to save and invest wisely.

  We can learn to make money work for us, rather than working for money. We must learn to accumulate and use assets, rather than continuing to collect liabilities.

Later in the book, I will talk in detail about each of these points. But before I do that, I want to establish some basic concepts and challenge your thinking!

COMMON SENSE IDEAS

1. The Church is not a bank; it does not exist to solve the financial problems of individuals. The purpose of a church is to teach principles from God's Word so that *individuals are empowered to solve their own problems.*

2. The natural mind *sees* things; the spiritual mind *looks into* things.

3. The solution to a problem is rooted within the problem itself.

4. New action must be taken to change a situation; doing the "same old, same old" will not change a financial situation.

5. It is essential to depart from what's known to get what's wanted out of life.

6. The story of the widow woman included a miracle, but it was not a "financial miracle." God did not cancel the woman's debt. He showed her the way out of the situation.

7. No spiritual gimmicks exist for getting out of debt.

THE AMOUNT OF
MONEY POSSESSED
DOES NOT CHANGE
THE WAY A PERSON
THINKS ABOUT MONEY.
THOSE UNDISCIPLINED
BEFORE HAVING MONEY
***WILL* BE UNDISCIPLINED**
AFTER HAVING MONEY.

Chapter 2

The Myth of "Financial Miracles"

I believe a financial crisis exists in our world. That is why I am writing this book. People are going into debt at amazing rates. **This** concerns me. I do not have anything against debt specifically, but I do not want to see the Body of Christ mismanage the money that God has given us. I want us to avoid the mistakes of the world—not repeat them!

Let's take a look at some startling facts about the world's financial health.

MANY PEOPLE LIVE ONE PAYCHECK FROM BANKRUPTCY

While each country in the world is facing its own economic turmoil, the United States is facing unprecedented economic difficulties. People's financial security blankets are being pulled out from under them. Let me share some statistics with you.

The *Washington Post* (Jan. 12, 2004) reported the following in an article titled "Consumer Debt Grows at an Alarming Rate":

- The average American household owes $9,000 in credit card

debt. If that figure is adjusted for the 40% who pay their bills in full each month, the average credit card debt owed per household for the remaining 60% rises close to $13,000.

- An all-time high of 1.6 million households declared bankruptcy in 2003.

- American household debt, excluding mortgages, has doubled in fewer than 10 years. It was 1 trillion dollars in 1994 and topped 2 trillion dollars in 2003.

- Three out of every five American families carry credit card debt.

- In 2002, the average household consumer debt produced $1,700 in finance charges and fees.

- CardWeb.com estimates that among American households with at least one credit card, there are 16.7 credit cards on average held by the household (that includes 6 bank credit cards, 8 retail cards, and 2 or 3 debit cards).

These statistics are staggering. A financial crisis is brewing. I believe we are living in a mirage of wealth. I want to help people find their way back to reality—in a common-sense way!

I believe the solution to these types of financial difficulties is rooted in changing the way people think about money and work. I *don't* believe the solution to these types of financial problems lies in the myths that are being taught in some churches today. Let me explain further.

THERE ARE TOO MANY MYTHS ABOUT FINANCES IN THE CHURCH TODAY

Many Christians find themselves in the financial troubles described above. They are *desperate* for help! Like the widow woman in the story in 2 Kings, they come to church for help when they are in financial trouble.

And what do they hear? They hear empty "promises" from the pulpit. Preachers promise them "financial miracles" and talk about "supernatural debt reduction." Such preachers are feeding off people's fears. Instead of giving people proper instruction, they lead them into religious deception.

Preachers "promise" something like this: "Just give in this offering, and God will work a miracle and you will be debt-free in no time." Or, something like: "Yes, I hear God telling me that there are 50 of you here tonight, and that if you will run to the front right now and each give $1,000, that God will cause your debts to be cancelled within 30 days." Now I ask you, if giving really caused God to work a "financial miracle," why would they need *you* to give to *them*?

Why wouldn't *they* be giving to *your* financial problem, so God could work a "financial miracle" for them? Why is giving to these preachers the only way to receive "financial miracles?"

EXPOSING THE MYTH OF "FINANCIAL MIRACLES"

I want to take some time and look in more detail at this idea of "financial miracles" that some have been teaching the Body of Christ. Some people talk about "supernatural debt reduction" or "supernatural debt cancellation" or "miracle offerings." I call all of these the "myths of financial miracles." I hope that those who have preached these things thought they were trying to help people. But, I don't believe these teachings are scriptural. This is why I call them myths. They may sound good, but there is no foundation for them in the Bible.

This type of "financial miracle" **teaching** has become deceptive. It is so sad to see that only desperate and financially strapped people are buying into these myths. It happens because they have a desperate need for money.

Desperation leads to deception!

I see this as being similar to a drowning person. People who are drowning are desperate to grab anything they think will save them. Lifeguards know they **must** wait until the person drowning quits struggling in order to save them. People who are struggling financially will grasp at anything to save themselves, even though it may be deceptive. The truth is that only when they quit grasping in desperation, and start thinking differently, will their situation change.

Satan's **greatest** goal is to trap us – **to** keep us from fulfilling the will of God for our lives. In the area of money, he deceives us into thinking that we can just sit back, doing nothing, and believe that God will turn our financial situations around all by Himself. This deception leads us to think that we can *just pray* our way into more money or *just give* our way into more money. Friends, it just does not work that way!

Preachers need to teach principles of financial responsibility so people **can be** equipped to handle their finances well. Teaching principles on how to manage money wisely is not as flashy—nor does it promise results as quickly—as preaching about mythical "financial miracles." But, it is the right thing to do.

To keep us from being deceived, I want to take a look at some of the myths people are being told are "financial miracles."

THE MYTH OF GIVING TO GET A "FINANCIAL MIRACLE"

Some preachers are saying you can just "give your way out of debt." I do not believe it is that simple. There is more to it than *just* giving and getting a "financial miracle."

Please do not misunderstand what I am saying. I believe in giving! But our giving must be in line with Scripture. Giving is part of God's plan for man, but God must be the One who directs our giving. We must not allow ourselves to be manipulated by a hollow promise coming from a pulpit.

Look with me at the following verses in THE MESSAGE Bible, 2 Corinthians 9:6-7:

> *"Remember a stingy planter gets a stingy crop; a lavish planter gets a lavish crop. I want each of you to* ***take plenty of time to think it over****, and* ***make up your own mind*** *what you will give. That will* ***protect you*** *against sob stories and arm-twisting. God loves it* ***when the giver delights in the giving****."*

Notice what I emphasized in the bold print. God wants us

There is no quick fix for irresponsible spending habits!

to take plenty of time to think over what we are going to give. That doesn't sound like He wants us to give when our emotions have been stirred up in a service, does it? The Apostle Paul, inspired by the Holy Spirit, exhorts us to give ***after*** we have taken plenty of time to think it over. He wants us to ***"make up our own mind,"*** rather than just blindly doing what some preacher tells us to do.

Why do you think these instructions are here? If we read on, we will see. Paul makes it plain for us. He wants *"**to protect us** against sob stories and arm twisting!"* Did you see that? The Spirit of God, writing through Paul, wants to protect us from being emotionally manipulated into giving money.

Paul says he wanted to protect people from *"sob stories and arm twisting"* in the 1st century, and I want to protect people in the 21st century from the same thing. I am concerned because I see too many people being manipulated into giving today—all based on a hollow promise.

The Bible says that our giving should be purposeful—after thinking and, I believe, after praying about it. We should not give under pressure or manipulation.

When I hear preachers today telling people the amount of money to give in an offering, I think about this Scripture. God does not want preachers to be telling people how much to give.

There is another Scripture in THE MESSAGE Bible that gets even more pointed. I share this not to accuse any preacher, but to make us aware that even Jesus knew that not every person who preaches the Bible has the best motive when they are preaching. The Scripture is Matthew 7:15-20:

> *"[15]Be wary of false preachers who smile a lot, dripping with practiced sincerity. Chances are they are out to rip you off some way or other. Don't be impressed with charisma; look for character. [16-20]Who preachers are is the main thing, not what they say. A genuine leader will never exploit your emotions or your pocketbook."*

Wow! What a warning Jesus gives to us. There were preachers like that back then, and there are some around today, more than 2,000 years later. Let's be aware!

God wants us to take time to think about our giving. I believe He wants us to *ask Him* how much to give and not let preachers *tell us* how much to give. We should give with delight because we have asked God what He wants us to give. After doing that, we simply are obeying *His instructions*—not giving in response to pressure or manipulation or empty promises. When we give in response to God's instructions, we can expect His blessings in our lives!

THE MYTH OF "WEALTH TRANSFER"

Now, I need to get more specific. I may make a few people uncomfortable with what I am about to say, but I want to tell the truth and shame the devil.

I have actually heard some preachers tell people to pray and believe that God will cause banks to make mistakes and put money into their bank accounts. Or, these preachers offer other empty promises similar to this. I have heard some of them even quote a Scripture to support their idea. They will preach from Proverbs 13:22, which states, "*...wealth of the sinner is stored up for the righteous.*"

These preachers make it sound like God has put wealth into sinners' hands and then, at some time in the future, He is going to siphon it out of the sinners' hands and put it into the hands of Christians. Generally those who preach this message imply that Christians just need to sit around and pray and believe that this will happen. Is that what this Scripture really means?

- NO! I don't believe it does. Only irresponsible people have a mentality of wanting something that will cost them nothing.

GOD IS NOT ROBIN HOOD!

Can I tell you the truth? Proverbs 13:22 does not mean that God will "supernaturally" put money into our bank accounts, while we sit and do nothing but pray and believe that someone at the bank will make a big mistake. Do you know what praying like that is? It is witchcraft prayer! It is a work of the flesh! God won't answer prayers like that!

Let me tell you something. If a bank makes a mistake and puts money into our accounts by accident, we need to tell the bank about that mistake. If we don't, we become thieves and liars. We are stealing someone else's money. God is not Robin Hood. He will not steal from the rich and give it to us. And He does not want

His people becoming thieves. I will no longer sit back and let some preachers tell lies like this!

Maybe some of these preachers are well meaning. But the truth is, *they are deceived!* There is no scriptural basis for this kind of teaching. God will not honor this type of teaching, nor will He answer these types of prayers. This is what I call "prophelying" to the people of God.

DID THE CHILDREN OF ISRAEL RECEIVE A TRANSFER OF WEALTH?

I have heard some preachers say we can believe for a "wealth transfer," like the one that happened to the children of Israel when they left Egypt. They are thinking about Exodus 3:21-22, where it states:

> *"[21]And I will give this people favor in the sight of the Egyptians; and it shall be, when you go, that you shall not go empty-handed. [22]But every woman shall ask of her neighbor, namely, of her who dwells near her house, articles of silver, articles of gold, and clothing; and you shall put them on your sons and on your daughters. So you shall plunder the Egyptians."*

Many people use this Scripture to support their idea that God is going to take money from sinners and put it into the hands of Christians.

I want us to stop and think about this. Yes, the children of Israel walked out of Egypt with a lot of the Egyptian wealth. But, have you ever stopped to think that Israel had worked for Pharaoh for 430 years without a paycheck? So when we read this story, remember that God was correcting an injustice by giving them what they worked for over the course of 430 years. It is called "payback" I believe—with interest! We cannot claim that as a promise from God for us. That payback was for a specific situation.

If we work for a company for 20, 30, or 40 years and we receive wonderful stock options that make us rich when we retire, I am all for that. We have worked to earn that. But, simply sitting on the front steps of a company for 20, 30, or 40 years, just praying for stock options, is not going to make us rich. That is ridiculous! It is just as ridiculous to believe that God will cause a bank to make a mistake and put money in our account. Or, to believe that just because we give some preacher some money that God will "supernaturally" cancel our debts. That is what I call foolishness!

I always challenge people with this thought: If we think money comes by praying, then we need to invite Bill Gates to bring his intercessors to our churches and teach us how to pray to get the kind of money he has. This may sound somewhat comical, but you get my point. The truth is, Bill Gates has used his God-given ability to become a problem-solver by creating a software company that helps people run their computers effectively. He made his money by working and providing a solution to problems.

WHAT IS A REAL MIRACLE?

Now that I have exposed the deception about these so-called "financial miracles," let me share with you the truth about what the Bible really teaches about miracles. I do not want to see people deceived. The only way to prevent deception is to know the truth.

ERROR IS NOTHING MORE THAN A TRUTH CARRIED TO AN EXTREME

I believe God is a miracle-working God. But our society uses this word "miracle" so frequently in casual conversations that it has lost its true meaning. We label things as miracles when they're not. For example, we have "Miracle Whip®"; we call something a "miracle drug" or a "miracle cleaner." There was even a television show called "Miracles."

We are not much different in the church today. We think that anything good that happens to us is a miracle. Much misunderstanding exists in the church when it comes to miracles. It is very sad to see so many Christians confused concerning the difference between a miracle, which is God supernaturally intervening in a situation, and a blessing, which we experience as a result of our obedience to God's Word.

What is a miracle? A miracle is God working beyond our ability to get something done for us. A miracle is a temporary interruption in the normal course of events. God never intended for us to live from miracle to miracle. He may perform a miracle for us, but He never intends for us to stay in the same situation after the miracle that we were in before the miracle.

A MIRACLE IS NOT PERMANENT

A miracle is not permanent. A miracle is instant. It is God interrupting time as we know it to do something that cannot be explained by mankind. A miracle occurs when God intervenes in a situation *temporarily* to do something we could never do on our own.

When God performs a miracle, we have *nothing* to do with it. It happens because God intervenes in our circumstances in a supernatural way. A miracle temporarily interrupts the ordinary course of nature. We never know when a miracle is going to happen, and we never know if a miracle is going to happen again. We cannot dial up a miracle anytime we want one.

I am convinced that God performs miracles so that we will change the way we think. A miracle without a corresponding change in our thinking will not profit us in the long run. Without a change in our thinking, we soon will find ourselves back in the same situations that created a need for the miracle.

Let's take a look at some real miracles in the Bible.

GOD'S MIRACLES BRING ABOUT HIS PURPOSES—NOT OUR PLEASURE!

Let's start with a miracle in the New Testament. Take a look with me at Luke 1:26-38. In these verses we read about the angel Gabriel appearing to Mary to tell her she is going to bear a child. We know that child was Jesus. His birth was a miracle because Mary did not have a husband—nor did she have sexual intercourse with Joseph to have this baby. (The Bible calls her a virgin—something that our society does not value much today, but something that is very precious in God's eyes.) So, how does a virgin have a baby without having sexual intercourse with a man? Only by a miracle. Mary could do nothing by herself to get pregnant. It is impossible for a woman to become pregnant all by herself. All she did was say "Yes" to God. God then performed the miracle.

There was another child born at this time—to Elizabeth and Zacharias (see Luke 1:5-25). Some people call what happened to them a miracle, but it really isn't. They were old, but they were not too old to conceive a baby. God just expected them to do what a husband and wife do — have sexual intercourse to have a baby. They did not experience a miracle. They had sexual intercourse, and Elizabeth conceived. They did what they could do, because it did not require a miraculous intervention by God to conceive a baby. They were obedient, and God blessed them with a baby as a result. That is not a miracle!

Let me remind you, once again, what a miracle is. It is a supernatural intervention in the ordinary course of nature — a temporary suspension of the accustomed order of things. It is the Spirit of God entering into time, as we know it, and instantly creating what cannot be seen or understood by the human mind.

Now, do you understand the difference between the miracle that God performed for Mary and how God blessed Elizabeth and Zacharias? Mary could not have a baby by herself. She needed divine intervention. Elizabeth and Zacharias did not require divine intervention. They simply had to obey God and do what they could do. They did not experience a miracle. They received a blessing from God.

Miracles fulfill God's agenda in the earth.

I want you to pay close attention to what happened in the life of the Virgin Mary. First, she had a supernatural visitation. Second, the Holy Spirit was the divine influence in the miracle. Mary did not have sexual intercourse with a man in order to become pregnant (as Elizabeth did). The Holy Spirit is involved in every miracle that happens on this earth. Third, the miracle was to advance the purposes of God. It was not to benefit Mary individually. It advanced God's kingdom. Miracles always advance the purposes of God, not our own selfish desires.

GO AND SIN NO MORE!

Let's look at another miracle in the New Testament. Remember the man at the pool of Bethesda (see John 5:1-15). Jesus healed him…miraculously! Jesus spoke to the man and he was healed after 38 years of sickness. THAT is a miracle. But after the miracle, Jesus gave him a very specific instruction. Look at John 5:14:

> *"[14]Afterward Jesus found him in the temple, and said to him, 'See, you have been made well. Sin no more, lest a worse thing come upon you.'"*

Jesus made it clear that the man needed to do something different after he received his miracle. Jesus' instruction to him was to *"sin no more."* That means he had to change the way he was living. Jesus also told him that if he did not change the way he was living, something worse would come on him. Is that what Jesus wanted? No. But our actions always have consequences. And Jesus wanted this man to keep his healing. So He instructed him to sin no more—or to change his way of living.

Notice that Jesus demanded that this man change his way of living after he had experienced the miracle. The only way we change our way of living is to change the way we think. I believe that is God's heart for anyone who experiences a miracle. Too many people ask God to perform financial miracles for them and then keep thinking the same way about their finances. I can tell you it just doesn't work that way!

Sometimes it amazes me when I hear people talk about changing their lives but never considering the process they must go through to get what they want. If you want something new out of life, you will have to change the way you think in order to handle the thing you desire. Consider the example of a wife whose husband is not doing right. The wife prays for him and God intervenes, and the husband begins to change and starts doing things right. The wife will not be able to handle the new circumstances, if she doesn't change along with him.

The children of Israel are an example of this. Look at two verses with me. Numbers 14:3-4 states:

> *"[3]Why has the LORD brought us to this land to fall by the sword, that our wives and children should become victims? Would it not be better for us to return to Egypt?" [4] So they said to one another, "Let us select a leader and return to Egypt."*

After they cried out to God to change their condition, God brought them out of bondage from the Egyptians and took them into the land of promise. But when they got there, they could not handle the change. And why couldn't they handle it? Because they did not change their mentality. They still had the mentality of victims.

You will only live at the level of your thinking.

I want you to notice in these verses of Scripture, how God provided what the Israelites wanted, but they could not enter into it. They could not enter into the promise because of something on the outside. It was not because there were giants in the land. It was something much more subtle. It was because their thinking was not at the level to handle the promise. You see, friends, to live in the land of abundance, you will need to have an abundance mentality.

GOD PERFORMED MIRACLES FOR THE CHILDREN OF ISRAEL

Let me repeat myself. I believe God is a miracle-working God. I also believe that God does not work miracles just to bail us out of difficult financial situations. Let's take a look at God's relationship with the children of Israel as an example.

The children of Israel experienced the manifestation of the working of miracles as God was delivering them from Egypt's bondage. Deuteronomy 29:2-3 states:

> *"[2]Now Moses called all Israel and said to them: 'You have seen all that the LORD did before your eyes in the land of Egypt, to Pharaoh and to all his servants and to all his land—[3]the great trials which your eyes have seen, the signs, and those great wonders.'"*

Here Moses reminds the people of all that God did for them when they escaped from Egypt. Remember, Israel had no way to escape from the slavery in which Pharaoh held them. Israel was Pharaoh's work force. Can you imagine having two million low-paid workers to do whatever you wanted? Pharaoh was not going to let them go—without God's intervention.

So God performed miracles on behalf of His people to get Pharaoh to let them go. Look at this list of miracles God performed through Moses in order to set His people free:

- God turned the Nile River into blood and then turned it back into water (Exodus 7:14-25).
- God caused frogs, lice, and flies to overwhelm the land. The flies did not enter the children of Israel's homes, while they swarmed the homes and the lands of the Egyptians (Exodus 8).
- The Egyptian's livestock became sick and died, but God spared the livestock of the children of Israel (Exodus 9:1-7).
- God caused darkness to cover the land of Egypt, while He kept light in the houses of the Israelites (Exodus 10:21-29).
- The firstborn children of all of the Egyptians died, while the children of Israel were all spared (Exodus 11:1-12:30).

The children of Israel did not have anything to do with these miracles. God intervened in their situation temporarily in order to bring about their freedom from Egypt.

After these miracles, Pharaoh thought he had had enough, and he let the children of Israel leave the land of Egypt. But then he changed his mind and sent his whole army after them. Again, God performed a miracle on behalf of the Israelites. God split the

Red Sea while the Israelties walked through it, and then caused it to go back into its place. The whole Egyptian army drowned in the Red Sea (see Exodus 14). Again, the children of Israel had nothing to do with this miracle.

Now let's go back to our passage of Scripture in Deuteronomy 29, and we will see that God sustained the children of Israel with miracles while they were in the desert. Deuteronomy 29:5 states:

> *"5And I have led you forty years in the wilderness. Your clothes have not worn out on you, and your sandals have not worn out on your feet."*

Now that is a miracle! Can you imagine wearing clothes for 40 years without wearing out? Or wearing shoes that do not wear out in 40 years? As a parent, having raised two grown boys, I KNOW that is a miracle.

I want to repeat this: *the children of Israel did not have anything to do with these miracles.* All they did was put their clothes on each day and put their shoes on each day. GOD made their shoes and their clothes last. He had to do this. There was no Wal-Mart or local department store in the wilderness where they could get clothes. God had to intervene miraculously by interrupting the natural course of deterioration to keep their clothes from wearing out.

We also know that God fed them supernaturally throughout their travels in the wilderness. Exodus 16 tells the story of the way God fed the children of Israel with manna and quail. Each night, quails came into the camp, so they would have meat. Every morning, dew covered the ground around the camp. When the dew lifted, manna was left behind. Now tell me, when was the last time birds flew into your back yard each evening so you could cook them for dinner? And when was the last time bread was left on your grass after the dew lifted in the morning? That probably has not happened in your lifetime, has it?

These are miracles! God intervened in these situations to do something the children of Israel could not possibly do for themselves. The wilderness could not sustain several million people each day for 40 years without God's intervention!

GOD EXPECTS US TO USE THE OPPORTUNITIES HE GIVES US

Now here is the key point I want to make. God sustained the children of Israel the whole time they were in the desert, through the working of miracles. But when the children of Israel got to the place where they could take care of themselves, the miracles stopped. Look at Joshua 5:11-12:

> *"[11]And they ate of the produce of the land on the day after the Passover, unleavened bread and parched grain, on the very same day. [12]Then the manna ceased on the day after they had eaten the produce of the land; and the children of Israel no longer had manna, but they ate the food of the land of Canaan that year."*

When the children of Israel arrived in the Promised Land, they could eat the food in that land; they could farm and raise food for themselves. So the manna and the quail stopped. No more manna or quail appeared from that day forward. Why? Because God expected them to become responsible and start producing for themselves after they were delivered from bondage.

God provided for them for the whole time they were in the wilderness. But once they reached their Promised Land, He expected them to begin to use their abilities and produce in their new country. He wanted them to be dependent on Him spiritually, but to become independent of the circumstances in that land. He wanted them to establish their economic independence in a new country.

Let me interject a thought here. The wealth of a country is not measured by how much money it has in its treasury. It is measured by its **Gross National Product (GNP)**:

- Gross—the overall or total amount.
- National—the involvement of the population.
- Product— the substance and productivity of the people's creativity.

No country can have a strong economy if the country's people are not industrious and innovative. This makes the difference between those countries that are productive and those that are not.

When the children of Israel arrived where God wanted them to be, He gave them the responsibility to work so they could build a nation. They had to put their ability to work. They had to create their own Gross National Product. They could no longer rely on the miracles they had in the wilderness.

"FINANCIAL MIRACLES" ARE NOT THE WAY TO CHANGE OUR FINANCIAL SITUATION

Proverbs 28:19 in the New Century Version states:

"[19]Those who work their land will have plenty of food, but the ones who chases empty dreams instead will end up poor."

The myth of "financial miracles" is like chasing pipe dreams. The Bible will never teach us a "microwave approach" to life—something that happens quickly with not much cost to us. And, that is exactly what "financial miracle" teaching is really about.

Those who are teaching on "financial miracles" don't recognize that the ones being taught need more than just a prayer or an empty promise to turn their situations around. Many people facing financial crises need their minds renewed concerning their financial dealings.

Let's just imagine that I pray for you to get a "financial miracle"—which I would not do because I don't believe in this. But let's just imagine that I did. And, let's also imagine that as a result of this "financial miracle," all your bills were wiped out at once. There would still be no guarantees that you would stay out of debt in the future. That's because the amount of money you got in this imaginary "financial miracle" would not change your thinking about money. Because you were undisciplined *before* you got a so-called "financial miracle," you would still be undisciplined *after* you got a "financial miracle"—and it would only be a matter of time before you lost all the money again.

Proverbs 13:11 in The New Century Version states:

"[11]Money that comes easily disappears quickly, but money that is gathered little by little will grow."

Therefore, a "financial miracle" should never be your primary focus, if you have undisciplined spending habits. The best thing you can do is to change your thinking, which will change your financial habits.

Look at what Proverbs 28:22 in the New Century Version states:

"22Selfish people are in a hurry to get rich."

The verse does not say that this person is in a hurry to learn the principles of wealth. It says he is in a hurry to get rich. You can find this kind of mentality roaming throughout our churches today. Too many people are just looking for ways to get rich quick. I believe it's time for us, as the people of God, to discipline ourselves in financial matters and to quit looking for these myths that we mistakenly call "financial miracles" as a way out of financial crises.

GOD DOES NOT RUN A SOCIALIST KINGDOM

Nowhere in the Bible will you find that God runs His kingdom like a socialist country. The present-day teaching on "financial miracles" is like something you'd find in a socialist country. In a socialist country, the government takes money from the hard-working people who earned it and redistributes it to the poor. God's kingdom operates differently. It operates based on personal responsibility.

I have a personal belief that Genesis 1 and 2 always has been God's plan for the human race. In my understanding of redemption, God sent His Son to restore mankind to His original plan, laid out in these two chapters. In His original plan, God gave mankind (men and women) the management responsibility of this planet. I believe that is still His plan today.

Let's go back to God's original plan. Look at Genesis 1:28 with me. It states:

> *"[28]Then God **blessed** them, and God said to them, 'Be **fruitful** and **multiply**; fill the earth and **subdue** it; have **dominion** over the fish of the sea, over the birds of the air, and over every living thing that moves on the earth.'"*

Let's look at what God established for mankind in these verses, because it is the pattern by which He designed us to live.

First, He blessed Adam and Eve. So many times when we say God blessed a person, we mean that God gave that person something—an item, generally something material. But is that what He did when He blessed Adam and Eve? I don't see that in this Scripture.

God did not give Adam and Eve any material *things that were fully developed. They had only the raw materials*. When He blessed them, God *empowered* them. That is what "to be blessed" means. To "bless" means to empower. When God blessed them, He gave them the ability to produce. He blessed them with creative power. He gave them a world in which there was an abundance of resources. You could say God gave Adam and Eve a world of opportunities!

Second, He commanded them to be fruitful and multiply. Now think with me. What does it mean to be fruitful and multiply? Yes, I do know that it means they were to have children, but I believe it means more than that. If that phrase refers only to children, then God would have expected Adam and Eve to do nothing more than have sexual intercourse and have babies. But when you and I stop to think about it, we know that is not *all* God wanted them to do.

To be fruitful and multiply means that God wanted them to *do something*. To be fruitful and multiply implies God wanted them to increase. God wanted them to produce something with the talents and abilities He had given them. God did not expect them to just sit around and pray for Him to do everything. He gave them an abundance of raw material, and He expected them to be productive.

Third, He told them to subdue and have dominion. The words "subdue and have dominion" mean to tread down or to conquer something. God expected Adam and Eve to use what He had put in the earth. (I am not saying He told them to abuse it, but to use it.) He wanted them to discover all that He had put in the earth and put it to good use. Everything that you and I use today was present when God created the earth. He commanded Adam and Eve to get to work discovering all that He had put here for us to use and to be productive.

God created the Garden, put Adam and Eve in it as His representatives, and expected them to work there. In God's original plan, He expected us to work and to produce what we need. He did not intend for us to just sit around and wait for Him to give us what we need. He wanted us to use the abilities He had given us. And He planned to reward us for using those abilities.

WE NEED TO UNDERSTAND WHAT MONEY REALLY IS

What is money? It is a medium of exchange in our world. We exchange our money for solutions to our problems. We give our money to people who have the solutions to our problems. So, I propose that the best definition of money is that it is a reward we get for solving problems in this life.

When you use your talents and abilities to solve a problem for someone else, you are rewarded with money. That is what your salary really is. Your employer has a problem. Your employer needs to get something done and needs your abilities to do it. You use your abilities to solve his problem and you are rewarded with money—your salary.

Let me expand on this thought with a simple example from everyday life. After you finish a day's work, you are hungry. Your hunger is a problem that needs to be solved. You can solve that problem in several ways. But let's say you stop at the grocery store on your way home, and you pick up some food. The food you buy is the solution to your problem. But, that food would not have been there without the owner opening the store. As you leave the store, you give him money for the food. Why? Because he solved a problem you had. You rewarded him with money because he solved a problem for you.

That is the way life works. We solve problems, and we get rewarded with money.

That is the way God set it up from the beginning. God did not put the food in the Garden in Adam's mouth. He had to work to get it. And he was rewarded for his effort. God started this process, and He still approves it today. He wants us to work!

Money is a reward for solving problems.

God never told us to pray for money.

God's kingdom is designed so that we will have to solve some kind of problem to earn money. We earn money because we solve problems. The more problems we solve—or the more difficult the problems we solve—the more money we make. God created us all with the ability to solve specific types of problems. When we use those God-given abilities to solve problems, we are rewarded with money.

Money is not a reward for praying or "being spiritual" and just believing God for money. Let's quit being nonproductive and go to work using the abilities God has given us so we can produce the money to meet our needs in life.

COMMON SENSE IDEAS

1. There are no quick fixes for financial problems.
2. God does not create money; financial miracles are a myth.
3. Desperation leads to deception.
4. God wants us to give, not because we have been emotionally manipulated, but because we have asked Him, then we have obeyed Him.
5. God will not "supernaturally" put money into bank accounts while we sit and do nothing but pray.
6. God is not Robin Hood.
7. Miracles are when we work beyond our ability to get something done for us, when God interrupts time to do something that cannot be explained by mankind. They are not permanent.
8. Living occurs at the level of individual thinking.
9. The amount of money we have does not change our thinking. People who are undisciplined before having money will be undisciplined after having money.
10. God's original plan for mankind is clearly stated in Genesis 1 and 2.
11. Money is a reward for solving problems.

IF A PERSON'S THINKING IS
NOT RIGHT, MORE MONEY WILL NOT BE THE ONLY SOLUTION TO FINANCIAL
DIFFICULTIES.

Chapter 3

Get Wisdom and Common Sense

We need wisdom rather than mythical "financial miracles"!

As we established in the last chapter, a "financial miracle" is a myth! For something to be a miracle, God has to intervene in the natural course of life and do something extraordinary. In order for something to be a "financial miracle," God would have to "create" money. You and I both know that God does not create money. The Federal Reserve Bank was given the responsibility to print money and put it into circulation. If God created money for you, it would be counterfeit, because all the money that is in circulation is printed with a unique number that is kept by the Federal Reserve Bank. And, if you spent that counterfeit money, you would be **stealing—you would eventually be** arrested. God will not send money to you from heaven, because He has put all of the resources necessary for man's existence in the earth. For God to create money and give it to you would be against the laws He has established for mankind. And God will not violate His own laws.

WE LIVE IN A UNIVERSE OF LAWS GOVERNED BY A SYSTEM OF ORDER

One of the laws that governs this universe, when it comes to prosperity, is how you use your ability. Deuteronomy 8:18 (NIV) states:

"[18]But remember the LORD your God, for it is he who gives you the ability to produce wealth, and so confirms his covenant, which he swore to your forefathers, as it is today."

God has given every one of us abilities. Those abilities are locked inside of us in something we call *potential.* God wants our abilities to move from nonproductive *potential* to *productive ability*. You could say our abilities need to move from potential energy to creative energy.

A story in the Gospel of Matthew shows how important our abilities are to God. Read the following with me from Matthew 25:14-15:

"[14]For the kingdom of heaven is like a man traveling to a far country, who called his own servants and delivered his goods to them. [15]And to one he gave five talents, to another two, and to another one, to each according to his own ability; and immediately he went on a journey."

With ability comes responsibility. Responsibility is simply responding to the ability within you. Ability creates a right of expectation from the One who has given us the ability. Because God has given us abilities, He can place a demand on us to develop and use those abilities. The greater the ability, the greater the demand. Luke 12:48 states:

"[48]For everyone to whom much is given, from him much will be required; and to whom much has been committed, of him they will ask the more."

When God gives us ability, He expects us to develop it. As we develop it, He gives us more ability. For everything in which we show ourselves responsible, we qualify for more. That principle is demonstrated in our passage in Matthew 25. Let's read verses 19 and 20:

> *"19 After a long time the lord of those servants came and settled accounts with them."*

In other words, the lord of these servants came back expecting the servants to give an account of what they had done with the money he had given them. Remember, with ability comes responsibility. The lord gave these servants something to work with, so he had a right to expect them to do something with it. Let's read on:

> *"20 So he who had received five talents came and brought five other talents, saying, 'Lord, you delivered to me five talents; look, I have gained five more talents besides them.'"*

His response to the ability that God had given him caused him to make a profit. He did not waste his ability; he put it to work. This servant understood that the lord had a right to expect him to produce something. This servant was not surprised or shocked by the lord's expectation. He was eager to give the lord a good report.

Now, look at the lord's response to this servant in verse 21.

> *"21 His lord said to him, 'Well done, good and faithful servant; you were faithful over a few things, I will make you ruler over many things. Enter into the joy of your lord.'"*

The second servant, who had received two talents, also understood the lord's right to expect productivity with the money he had been given. He returned to the lord with the same report as the first servant; he had doubled what he had been given. (That exchange is recorded in verses 22 and 23.)

But the third servant had a different attitude from the other two. Look at what he said to the lord when he returned (in verses 24-25):

> *"[24]Then he who had received the one talent came and said, 'Lord, I knew you to be a hard man, reaping where you have not sown, and gathering where you have not scattered seed. [25]And I was afraid, and went and hid your talent in the ground. Look, there you have what is yours.'"*

The key to this man's behavior was in his perception of the lord. He called him "a hard man." Why did he think that? Because he was deceived. He thought the lord did not have a right to expect a return. He thought the money was his and he could do whatever he wanted with it. He even accused the lord of trying to reap where he had not sown and of trying to gather a harvest where he had not sown seed! Do you see how deceived this servant was? The lord had given him the money, and the lord had every right to expect a return on what he had given. It was the servant's attitude that beat him; it was not the attitude of the lord that was the problem!

Notice that the praise the first two servants received from the lord was based on their faithfulness to increase the value of their ability in the market place. They did not increase the value of the money they had by sitting and praying or by giving it away. The value of the money increased because the first two servants went to work and used their abilities. Money will only come to you based on how you use your abilities. God established the laws of finances, and He expects us to abide by them. It is really a common-sense law. You sow your ability in the marketplace, and you reap a harvest of financial prosperity.

DOES MONEY ANSWER EVERYTHING?

We need to examine a verse in Ecclesiastes. Some preachers use this verse to justify their promises that God will bless us, if we just give our money to them. The last part of the verse in Ecclesiastes 10:19 states: *"Money answers everything."* Now I ask you, does money really answer *everything?* Solomon wrote this, and a lot of what he wrote was written with skepticism. If we take this verse out of its rightful setting, we can come to the wrong conclusion.

Money can answer everything in the material realm. But money cannot answer marriage problems. Money cannot buy your children's affection. Money cannot heal a broken heart. And sometimes all the money in the world cannot buy our health. And, contrary to popular belief, money cannot buy happiness.

We do need money in this world. We need money to function on this planet. But we need more than money. Money without wisdom will not answer life's problems. Proverbs 17:16 (NIV) states:

> *"Of what use is money in the hand of a fool, since he has no desire to get wisdom."*

Some people **spend** almost all their waking moments thinking about money. Most of those people think that all they need is more money. I want to challenge **this type of** thinking. They don't need more money; **they need** more wisdom to manage the money they have.

I believe Christians need to pray for wisdom when it comes to finances, rather than believe for God to bail them out of financial crises. In fact, it can be dangerous to get bailed out of a financial crisis. You can get out of financial trouble quickly, but if you have not learned anything about obedience and responsibility, your ignorance will **cause you to return to that trouble.**

I have seen this with so many people who have financial difficulties. They **receive** an increase in **salary, and** instead of managing the increase, they spend it. All **this does is create a** bigger deficit than they had before. More money is not always the answer for financial difficulty.

Let's look at James 1:5 from the New International Version. It states:

> *"[5]If any of you lacks wisdom, he should ask God, who gives generously to all without finding fault, and it will be given to him."*

I want you to notice that the Bible does not say here that if anyone lacks *money,* they **are** to ask God for it. It says we are to ask God for wisdom. I believe when it comes to finances, wisdom is better than getting "miracle" money.

Why do I say that? Because wisdom is the ability to apply the knowledge you **already possess** in practical ways. Wisdom is common sense in operation. Wisdom is the ability to foresee what is going to happen and prepare for it. Money *can* answer every material problem we face. However, if we do not have the wisdom to manage the money we earn, we will not **retain that** money to pay for our material needs.

WISDOM IS MORE VALUABLE THAN MONEY!

In God's economy, wisdom always has a higher value than money. So don't believe preachers that preach this easy way **of living, declaring** that money answers everything. Most of them try to get you to think that all you need is more money. **Again, let** me challenge that thinking. You most likely don't need more money; you just need the wisdom to manage the resources you already have.

Look with me at Proverbs 3:13-18 (New Living Translation). It states:

> *"[13]Happy is the person who finds wisdom and gains understanding. [14]For the profit of wisdom is better than silver, and her wages are better than gold. [15]Wisdom is more precious than rubies; nothing you desire can compare with her. [16]She offers you life in her right hand, and riches and honor in her left. [17]She will guide you down delightful paths; all her ways are satisfying. [18]Wisdom is a tree of life to those who embrace her; happy are those who hold her tightly."*

Did you notice what God said here? Wisdom clearly has more value than money. When we have wisdom, we will have all the money we need. The Bible states that the profit of wisdom is better than silver. In other words, having wisdom is better than having silver in our hands.

Notice also that in verse 15, the Bible states that *nothing* can compare with wisdom. *Nothing* compares to wisdom? That's what the Bible says. Why is that? Because when we have wisdom, we have the answer for every situation. When we have wisdom, we will never be without the tools **needed** to act wisely in all situations.

With the wisdom of God, we **are** able **to** understand the economic times in which we live. I believe the wisdom of God will allow us to see opportunities that other people do not see. When we see opportunities that no one else sees, we can prosper. We make the mistake of pursuing money **as** our primary concern, rather than making the pursuit of wisdom our primary concern.

These verses also make it clear that wisdom is something we must embrace and hold tightly (verse 18). Notice that *we* must embrace wisdom. And we must hold her tightly. Wisdom will not force itself upon us. We must be diligent in our pursuit of wisdom. We must choose to hold on to wisdom. That is why I have written this book. I want people to be equipped with wisdom to face—and overcome—the financial challenges of life. Hype and empty promises do not prepare you to face financial challenges. But wisdom will! Make wisdom your priority.

SOLOMON ASKED FOR WISDOM ...AND GOT RICHES!

Solomon was a man who knew the value of wisdom. Let's look at a very interesting exchange between God and King Solomon. This exchange is in 2 Chronicles 1:7-12, right after David died and Solomon had taken his place as king of Israel. Verse 7 states: *"On that night God appeared to Solomon, and said to him, 'Ask! What shall I give you?'"*

Wait! Did you see that? Solomon is just starting his reign as king of Israel. God appears to Solomon and tells him to ask Him for anything he wanted.

Can you imagine God showing up and saying to you, "Go ahead. Ask me for anything you want." What would you ask for if God gave you that opportunity? Many people facing financial difficulties would ask for **more** money. They think of their immediate need and ask God to meet **it. But** if all they got was money, they would soon spend it all and be back in the same place they were before God gave them the money.

Let's see what Solomon did. When given the chance to ask for anything, Solomon did not ask for money. Look at verses 8-10:

> *"[8]And Solomon said to God: 'You have shown great mercy to David my father, and have made me king in his place. [9]Now, O LORD God, let Your promise to David my father be established, for You have made me king over a people like the dust of the earth in multitude. [10]**Now give me wisdom and knowledge**, that I may go out and come in before this people; for who can judge this great people of Yours?'"*

Look at Solomon's response. Not the response of the average 21st century person, is it? Solomon asked for wisdom to judge God's people. He could have had *anything,* and he asked for wisdom and knowledge. Solomon's character (at this point in his life) was revealed in the choice he made.

Now look at God's response.

> *"[11]And God said to Solomon: 'Because this was in your heart, and you have not asked riches or wealth or honor or the life of your enemies, nor have you asked long life—but have asked wisdom and knowledge for yourself, that you may judge My people over whom I have made you king— [12]wisdom and knowledge are granted to you; and I will give*

> *you riches and wealth and honor, such as none of the kings have had who were before you, nor shall any after you have the like.'"*

God granted what Solomon asked for; God gave Solomon wisdom and knowledge. But that is not all that God gave Solomon. In addition to wisdom and knowledge, God gave Solomon riches and wealth and honor. In fact, He granted Solomon more riches and wealth and honor than anyone who ever lived! And I believe God gave him the riches because he asked for wisdom first.

WE MUST PURSUE WISDOM IN THE REALM OF FINANCES

Not everyone has the understanding needed to manage money wisely. Here is a good example. A well-known person, who had earned $300 million in his 20-year professional boxing career, recently filed for personal bankruptcy. Why? Because of his inability to manage what he had. Remember, Proverbs 13:11 (New Century Version) states: *"Money that comes easily disappears quickly. But money that is gathered little by little will slowly grow."* Another Scripture that backs this up is **Proverbs 21:16-17** (New Living Translation). It states:

Our character will always appear in the choices we make. Money just makes you more of who you are.

"[16]The person who strays from common sense will end up in the company of the dead, [17]who love pleasure become poor; wine and luxury are not the way to riches."

There is a saying, *"A fool and his money are easily parted."* We need wisdom to manage our money. If we do not manage well what we have, we do not qualify for more, because we will only mismanage it. To qualify for more, we must demonstrate that we know how to manage what we have!

WISDOM ALLOWS US TO MANAGE THE SEASONS IN LIFE

Sometimes we humans have the mentality that we will always live in a season of abundance. But the reality of life teaches us differently. Life is made up of different seasons. Ecclesiastes 3:1 states: *"To everything there is a season, a time for every purpose under heaven."*

Because life is made up of seasons, we should expect seasons of financial abundance and seasons of financial scarcity. The best thing you can do when you are in a season of abundance is manage your abundance wisely. Then, when the season of scarcity comes, you can diminish its effect on your life. That is just what Joseph did in Egypt.

JOSEPH USED WISDOM TO MANAGE THE FINANCES OF EGYPT

Let's look at Genesis 41, where we find the story of Pharaoh and his dreams. He had two of them, one about cows and one about heads of grain. He did not know what the dreams meant and looked for someone in Egypt to interpret the dreams.

This is where Joseph enters. Joseph was in prison. (He had been sent there innocently, having been falsely accused by Potiphar's wife.) While there, he interpreted a dream for Pharaoh's butler. The interpretation of the dream proved to be right, and the butler was restored to his post serving Pharaoh. When Pharaoh had his dreams, the butler remembered Joseph and told Pharaoh about him. Pharaoh called for Joseph to see if he could interpret his dreams.

Look with me at verses 15-16 of Genesis 41:

> *"15 And Pharaoh said to Joseph, 'I have had a dream, and there is no one who can interpret it. But I have heard it said of you that you can understand a dream, to interpret it.' 16 So Joseph answered Pharaoh, saying, 'It is not in me; God will give Pharaoh an answer of peace.'"*

Then Pharaoh told Joseph about his dreams, and God gave Joseph the interpretation. Through the dreams, God revealed that seven years of abundance would be followed by seven years of famine. Joseph, after interpreting the dream, also told Pharaoh what he should do. Not only did Joseph receive the interpretation, he also had the wisdom of God to deal with the situation. Look with me at Genesis 41:33-41:

> *"33 'Now therefore, let Pharaoh select a discerning and wise man, and set him over the land of Egypt. 34 Let Pharaoh do this, and let him appoint officers over the land, to collect one-fifth of the produce of the land of Egypt in the seven plentiful years. 35 And let them gather all the food of those good years that are coming, and store up grain*

under the authority of Pharaoh, and let them keep food in the cities. [36]Then that food shall be as a reserve for the land for the seven years of famine which shall be in the land of Egypt, that the land may not perish during the famine.' [37]So the advice was good in the eyes of Pharaoh and in the eyes of all his servants. [38]And Pharaoh said to his servants, 'Can we find such a one as this, a man in whom is the Spirit of God?' [39]Then Pharaoh said to Joseph, 'Inasmuch as God has shown you all this, there is no one as discerning and wise as you. [40]You shall be over my house, and all my people shall be ruled according to your word; only in regard to the throne will I be greater than you.' [41]And Pharaoh said to Joseph, 'See, I have set you over all the land of Egypt.'"

Now just think about this. When Pharaoh had a dream about what was going to happen to the economy of Egypt, he needed wisdom. He did not need a miracle; he needed wisdom. His staff, with all their education, **could not** help him prepare to deal with the situation. But Joseph knew what to do right away. Joseph's wisdom saved a whole nation from disaster. Pharaoh needed wisdom to deal with the situation he faced. And God gave Joseph the wisdom. God wants to provide the same type of wisdom for each of us today to deal with our situations.

GOD WANTS US TO WISELY MANAGE THE MONEY WE EARN

God wants us to use our God-given abilities to solve problems. Using our God-given abilities to solve problems will reward us with money. Once the money starts to flow into our hands, He wants us to manage the money wisely. When we manage money wisely, we will accumulate wealth so that we can establish God's covenant on the earth. That is in line with God's promise to us in Deuteronomy 8:18:

> "[18]*And you shall remember the LORD your God, for it is He who gives you power to get wealth, that He may establish His covenant which He swore to your fathers, as it is this day.*"

Notice that this Scripture does not say that God gives you the faith to believe for more money. It says God gives you the power or ability to *produce* wealth. *Producing* wealth means we must work for it. We cannot just pray it into existence. We must tap into our God-given potential.

WE MUST DEVELOP COMMON SENSE WITH OUR WISDOM

As I have said before, I like to take a common-sense approach to life. Wisdom and common sense work together. Let's look at some Scriptures that show the connection between wisdom and common sense. Proverbs 4:7-9 (The Living Bible) states:

> "[7]*Getting wisdom is the most important thing you can do! And with your wisdom, develop common sense and good judgment.* [8]*If you exalt wisdom, she will exalt you. Hold her fast and she will lead you to great honor;* [9]*she will place a beautiful crown on your head.*"

Notice, these verses admonish us to get wisdom. This

means we must do something to acquire wisdom. It will not just fall on us. Where you were born doesn't determine if you have wisdom or not. Your desire determines the amount of wisdom you will have. In other words, wisdom will not just appear for us. We cannot buy wisdom. We have to make a conscious decision to pursue wisdom. Wisdom comes only from God. It is through spending time in His presence—in prayer and in the Word—that we acquire wisdom.

And notice that, as we pursue wisdom, we are also told to develop common sense and good judgment. I believe that wisdom, common sense, and good judgment work together. However, wisdom, common sense, and good judgment are not the same as intelligence. I have met people who are very intelligent but who are not wise, nor do they have common sense or good judgment. They are prone to repeating the same mistakes over and over again. They self-destruct with their poor decisions. That is not wisdom.

As I have said before, common sense is not common today. In fact, it is rare in our 21st century. Too many people have settled for intelligence and have not moved deeper into wisdom and common sense. We can be intellectually smart, but not effective in the practicalities of life. Common sense makes us practical—we make wise decisions instead of impulsive ones. We think of the future rather than just the present. We live **practical but supernatural lives.** Our lives are directed by God's kingdom agenda and yet our lives are extremely relevant on the earth.

Look with me at some Scriptures that address our need for common sense. Proverbs 30:1-3 (New Living Translation) states:

> *"1 I am weary, O God; I am weary and worn out, O God. 2 I am too ignorant to be human, and I lack common*

sense. [3]I have not mastered human wisdom, nor do I know the Holy One."

Did you see that? This man (his name is Agur) says he is weary and worn out. Why? He says it is because he lacked common sense. WOW! That makes sense, doesn't it? When we lack common sense, we make life hard. I am convinced that God did not design life to be hard, but we make it hard because of the poor decisions we make. Agur had worn himself out because he did not practice common sense and because he had not mastered wisdom. I am convinced that if we just learned to live life from a common-sense point of view, life would be much more rewarding.

Look at another Scripture with me. Proverbs 21:16-17 (New Living Translation) states:

"[16]The person who strays from common sense will end up in the company of the dead. [17]Those who love pleasure become poor; wine and luxury are not the way to riches."

The lack of common sense drains the thrill of living from us. This Scripture tells us that we will wind up in the company of the dead when we do not apply common sense to life's problems. That is pretty straightforward. A lack of common sense leads us into the way of the dead. In other words, it can kill us.

Look again at verse 17. It says that common sense will keep us from falling for the unproductive ways in which the world gets trapped. A lack of common sense will cause us to love pleasure to the point that we become poor. Now, I am not against enjoying this life. However, too many people are pursuing short-term pleasures at the expense of their long-term well-being. If you do not die, you are going to live—and you are going to have to pay to live on this planet.

Ask yourself these questions: "Why do I want more money? Is it just to spend on short-term pleasures, or is there a greater purpose for the money I want?" If the only reason you want more money is to spend it on pleasure, I guarantee you will never have enough money. But if you see money from **God's** common-sense **perspective, which** means **seeing it as a tool rather than a goal, you** will always have the resources you need to do what God asks you to do in this life.

Notice that all these Scriptures insist we develop common sense. Why do we need to do that? Because common sense is not that common. If it were, everybody would possess it. We must develop common sense. It does not just happen. In fact, common sense is so uncommon that I wanted to write this book to make it common again. I want to see believers learn to manage money wisely and not fall for empty promises.

LET'S TAKE A COMMON SENSE APPROACH TO FINANCES

Now let's go back to our original story in 2 Kings 4 and examine the lessons that God has for us there. Remember, I want to **teach you how to have a** common-sense approach to keep the creditors from coming to your home.

I believe that the widow woman in the story in 2 Kings 4 received common-sense instructions from the man of God. As she obeyed those instructions, she came to a place where she could accumulate finances and then pay off her debt.

I want all of us to put these common-sense instructions to work in our lives so we can experience financial breakthroughs.

COMMON SENSE IDEAS

1. God does not create money.
2. We live in a universe of laws governed by a system of order.
3. God has given each person abilities, which He expects will be developed.
4. Responsibility is simply responding to the abilities God gives to each person.
5. Potential is the undeveloped ability within each person. God wants individuals to move from potential to productivity.
6. Money alone does not answer every problem.
7. We need wisdom to manage our finances, rather than to bail us out of financial crises.
8. Solomon asked for wisdom; he received wisdom AND riches.
9. Character appears in the choices people make.
10. Wisdom allows a person to manage seasons in life.
11. Joseph used wisdom to manage the affairs of Egypt.
12. Wisdom, common sense, and good judgment work together.
13. Elijah gave the widow woman common-sense instructions to turn her situation around.

WHAT WE
HAVE IN LIFE
DEPENDS
ON WHAT
WE DO WITH
WHAT'S IN
OUR HANDS.

Chapter 4

Being Responsible Qualifies Us for More

COMMON SENSE POINT # 1

We must be willing to take responsibility for our finances as well as the choices we make about how to manage them—we are where we are because of the choices and decisions we have made. We cannot blame God, the devil, or other people for where we are financially.

*"A certain woman of the wives of the sons of the prophets cried out to Elisha, saying, '**Your servant my husband** is dead, and you know that your servant feared the Lord. And **the creditor is coming** to take my two sons to be his slaves'" (2 Kings 4:1).*

Now, I want to return to our story about the widow woman in 2 Kings 4. We spent time looking at this story earlier in Chapter One. I showed you **previously** that Elisha did not take responsibility for the widow's financial situation. He did show her how *she* could change her situation. That is what I want to do in the next several chapters of this book, as well. I want people to be *free* from financial difficulties. I do not want to see them get a short-term fix for their poor money management, only to find themselves in financial difficulties again later.

In this chapter, I want us to look together at something many people miss. Many people do not see that something is wrong with the way their family has managed their finances. Let's take a few minutes to review the biblical story.

This is the story of a widow woman living at the time Elisha was a prophet to the nation of Israel. Her husband has died. She has two sons living at home. Her husband has left her in a terrible financial state. A creditor is coming to take her two sons to pay the debt.

If a creditor was coming to take your two **children** to pay your debt, do you think you would be panicking? I think we all would. So we can probably all sympathize with this woman. In fact, most of us in the church would expect the church to run to her rescue. "Let's bail her out! She is a widow, and we must take care of our own!" Yet, I don't think that is the best solution in a situation like this.

LET'S GO TO THE ROOT OF THE PROBLEM

Now don't get me wrong! I am not against helping people. I believe we, as Christians, are supposed to help people. But sometimes I **question whether** we really do ***help*** them. We tend to remove the immediate pain, but we do not help them in the long run. In other words, we solve a short-term problem, only to see people return to that same problem and condition in the future.

I think there is a better way. I think we **can** help people in the long run by *teaching them how to be responsible*. It may not be the most popular way to help, but I believe it is the best way.

I believe that Elisha **took** this opportunity to help this woman long-term **by teaching her how to be** responsible financially. And, may I suggest that Elisha **did this** because the woman's husband was *not* responsible with their finances?

Let's look at this more closely. Notice what this woman says about her husband. She says to Elisha, "Your servant, my husband, is dead, and you know that your servant feared the Lord." The widow's husband was Elisha's servant, and he feared the Lord. He was a man who was involved in the things of God.

Notice the order in which this woman referred to her husband and his relationship to Elisha. She *first* called him *"your servant." Then* she referred to him as her husband. Did you get that? To me, this implies that this man's priority was serving Elisha first, before he served his family. By calling her husband *"your servant,"* she was trying to make Elisha responsible for the situation. That is probably because she felt he had put the ministry before his family.

The widow's husband had to be somewhat mature in his faith in God. He was close to the most powerful man of God in those days. **He** was obviously well known to Elisha, because his widow did not have to mention his name for Elisha to know him. He had to walk in some level of spiritual maturity to have that kind of access to a man of God like Elisha.

GOD PROMISES TO BLESS THOSE WHO SERVE HIM

That causes me to wonder: how could this man die with so much debt? The Bible promises that God will provide for those who walk in the fear of God. Look at just a few of these promises with me:

- Proverbs 22:4 (New International Version) states: *"Humility and the fear of the LORD bring wealth and honor and life."*
- Psalm 34:9-10 (New King James Version) states: *"Oh, fear the LORD, you His saints! There is no want to those who fear Him. The young lions lack and suffer hunger; but* ***those who seek the LORD shall not lack any good thing****."*
- Psalm 37:18-19 (New King James Version) states: *"[18]The LORD knows the days of the upright,* ***And their inheritance shall be forever.*** *[19]They shall not be ashamed in the evil time, and* ***in the days of famine they shall be satisfied.****"* Verses 25-26 in the same chapter say, *"[25]I have been young, and now am old; Yet* ***I have not seen the righteous forsaken, nor his descendants begging bread.*** *[26]He is ever merciful,* ***and lends****;* ***And his descendants are blessed.****"*
- Psalm 112:1-3 (New King James Version) states: *"Praise the LORD! Blessed is the man who fears the LORD, Who delights greatly in His commandments. [2]His descendants will be mighty on earth; The generation of the upright will be blessed. [3]****Wealth and riches will be in his house,*** *And his righteousness endures forever."*

These Scriptures promise that the person who fears God and serves Him will be blessed—not just spiritually, but also with material things.

If you say "those are all Old Testament verses," let's look at what Jesus says. Jesus promises the same thing in Matthew 6:31-33, where He says:

> *"[31]Therefore do not worry, saying, 'What shall we eat?' or 'What shall we drink?' or 'What shall we wear?' [32]For after all these things the Gentiles seek. For your heavenly Father knows that you need all these things. [33]But seek first the kingdom of God and His righteousness, and all these things shall be added to you."*

Jesus promises if we seek His kingdom first, He will meet all of the needs we have in this life, including food, shelter, and clothing.

With these promises from God in mind, how could this man—who obviously gave great attention to the things of God—die with so much debt that the creditors would have to come to get his sons to pay the debt? Something is wrong with this picture. I know God kept His promises to this man, because God does not lie. That means that God provided for this man and his family. Yet at the end of life, this man left his family deeply in debt. Why? What could have gone wrong?

MISMANAGEMENT CONSUMES GOD'S BLESSINGS

I think the man mismanaged his resources. I believe this man was irresponsible. I believe he and his family made poor choices with the resources that God gave them. And that is why this man died and left his family in so much debt.

Why do I believe that? Because I see it all the time today. I see so many believers mismanaging their resources, they wind up in debt. They serve God; they are blessed by Him; yet, they are not managing the blessings they receive. They end up in severe financial crises. Let me tell you something. Being blessed by God does not relieve us of our responsibility to manage what He gives us.

I believe that this household is typical of many believers today. The Bible says that the *"sons of this world are more shrewd in their generation than the sons of light"* (Luke 16:8). Too many believers do not operate with wisdom when it comes to resources. We make poor decisions—living for the moment rather than planning for the future. The reason so many of us live this way is because we think this world is not our home, so we don't plan for our future here. I remember back in the early '70s (during what was called the "Jesus People Movement"), we thought we should not plan for the future because Jesus was coming soon. Therefore, many of us did not save for the future. Now, of course, many people from this era are older and have children whom they cannot send to college because their thinking about the future back at that time was wrong.

Being spiritual does not equate to being responsible! The Scriptures promising that God will bless us if we serve Him are not an entitlement that allows us to be irresponsible and mismanage what He gives us.

THE GOSPEL OF RESPONSIBILITY

Deuteronomy 30:19 (New Living Translation) states:

"Today I have given you the choice between life and death, between blessings and curses. I call on heaven and earth to witness the choice you make. Oh, that you would choose life, that you and your descendants might live!"

I believe in what I call "the Gospel of Responsibility." We are responsible for our choices. We have to live out the conse-

quences of our choices. The better choices we make, the be
consequences. The poorer the choices we make, the worse t
consequences we will face. It is up to us to make the right choices today to have the future we desire. We cannot mismanage what God gives us today and then expect Him to perform a "financial miracle" for us in the future.

Proverbs 10:4 states:

> *"[4]He who has a* ***slack hand*** *becomes poor, But the hand of the* ***diligent*** *makes rich. [5]He who* ***gathers in summer*** *is a wise son; He who* ***sleeps in harvest*** *is a son who causes shame."*

Notice that this Scripture shows the results of choices of those who are poor and those who are rich. The life**style** each and every one of us possesses was designed by the choices we **make.** It is our choices that make us who we **have become.**

Notice that being slack—which is another way **of saying that someone is irresponsible** causes us to become poor. On the other hand, if we are diligent and responsible, we will become rich. There is a condition for becoming rich. It is a word most people hate. Diligence precedes riches. Diligence qualifies us for riches. Laziness allows wealth to slip through our hands. This point is emphasized in the next verse. Notice in this verse that the wise person is working in the season of fruitfulness. Summer is a time of fruitfulness. This is a time when everything seems to grow, to become fruitful, and to produce. Summer represents a season of opportunity. It represents a season of growth and expansion for us.

This verse also talks about another person. It is the person who sleeps during the harvest. Harvest is the time to reap—not to re sleeping in harvest, you miss out on all that for. **Reaping** a harvest takes a lot of work. Many y can just sit back and the harvest will fall into out any effort of their own. But harvest is the time of th ense work—the longest hours, the hardest work, but the greatest reward. Farmers work harder and longer in harvest than at any other time of the year. They know that if they do not put in the time they need during the harvest, they will not reap the reward of the hard work they have already done.

Another thing to remember about harvest is this: farmers do not determine when the harvest occurs. **Farmers** keep watching their crops, and when the crops are ready, they drop everything else and start bringing in the harvest. Nothing matters as much as getting that harvest in, because the farmer realizes that this is the opportunity.

What you have in your life depends on what you do with what is in your hands.

If we are slack in managing the resources God gives to us, we will become poor, no matter how much comes into our hands. We must learn to manage the blessings He gives us. We must understand that when harvest comes in our lives, it is not so that we can use it all up. We must learn to manage it properly. We will talk more about this later, but first I want to address how we balance our responsibilities in life.

WE MUST BALANCE OUR RESPONSIBILITIES IN LIFE

You see, I believe the widow's husband did not balance his responsibilities properly between family and ministry. Many people have trouble balancing the different aspects of their lives—marriage, family, church, career, entertainment, etc. I want to challenge your thinking about having a strict priority for the various areas of your life. I want to suggest that each person must *balance* responsibilities—not put them into a strict order of priority.

Bryan Dawson, former CEO of Coca-Cola, in a speech, asked people to think of life as juggling five balls: "You name them: work, family, health, friends, and spirit. You will soon understand that work is a rubber ball. If you drop it, it will bounce back. But the other four balls—family, health, friends, and spirit—are made of glass. If you drop one of these, they will be irrevocably scuffed, marked, nicked, damaged, or even shattered. They will never be the same."

Let's turn back to the widow's statement. There is something disturbing about it. She said to the man of God, "Your servant, my husband." The order "your servant, my husband" indicates that in their household her husband was more loyal to the ministry of Elisha than he was to his family. I don't believe that God wants you to put ministry before your family. Nor do I believe that God wants your family to take priority over church. He wants to teach us how to balance our lives.

Balancing responsibilities in life is such an important issue that I want to specifically discuss three fundamental areas of personal responsibility: responsibility for our own self-government, responsibility for our family, and responsibility for our local church. Let's look first at the responsibility to govern our own individual life.

WE ARE RESPONSIBLE FOR OUR OWN SELF-GOVERNMENT

Being responsible for our own self-government starts with our individual relationship with God. To govern ourselves, we must develop our own individual relationship with God.

Let me be very clear here. When I say our individual relationship with God, I mean our time in fellowship with Him—not the time we spend serving Him. Many times, people make mistakes because they put serving God above their relationship with God. Too many times we get so busy in the work of the Lord that we forget the Lord of the work. That is when things get out of order in our lives.

Again, we must learn to develop our individual relationship with God. We must have our own prayer life. Husbands, you need to pray for your wives and children. Wives, you must pray for your husbands and children. The more we pray for one another, the less we will criticize one another. Take time during your day to pray. It will help you to function responsibly as an individual.

Prayer is seeking God's mind on your situation. Prayer is the time when we get God's perspective on our lives. Prayer is not telling God what you want Him to do. In your prayer time, ask God to reveal His will and plan for your life and the lives of your family members. Ask Him for the wisdom you need to manage your daily activities. Ask Him for the discernment you need to lead your

family. You can pray throughout the day—as you comm
over a walk at lunch, in the shower, or throughout an
of your day. Keep your heart open and attentive to God all day

As you develop the habit of seeking God about the everyday things in your life, you will learn to hear His instructions for your life. Then, when you act on the instructions He gives you, you will find yourself functioning responsibly. You will be governing yourself well. Then you will find that you are a blessing to your family, your church, and your place of work.

Find time during your day to read the Bible. The Bible is God's instruction manual for living. Think about cutting back on television or reading the paper or anything else that doesn't add value to your life. Ask God to show you the "time-wasters" in your life. We all have them. He will show you what these are in your life. Once this is revealed, use your time with God to fill yourself with His instructions.

One last thought on this: if your day or your thoughts are so busy that you do not have time for God, then you are not being led by God's Spirit. *He* is following *your* lead. If you find yourself in this situation, the most responsible decision you can make is to do the hard work of giving Him the time He needs to direct your life. (Notice, I am not telling you how much time to spend…that is something you work out with Him.) We must discipline ourselves to follow His lead, rather than taking the lead ourselves.

WE ARE RESPONSIBLE FOR GOVERNING OUR FAMILY

Our second responsibility is our relationship with our family—our spouse and our children. (If you are single, you should read this section; it will prepare you to be a better wife or husband.)

The best picture we have for marriages is God's love for His church. Our marriages should reflect the love of God. We must be willing to give up our selfish desires for our spouse. Marriage is a place where selfishness has to die. To be responsible in our marriage, we must learn to put our spouse's needs before our own. If every husband and wife did just this one simple thing, marriages would last a lifetime.

There is one word I use for a good marriage: ADAPT. A good marriage is built by learning to adapt each and every day. As husbands and wives learn to adapt to each other, their marriages become stronger, and our children see the model of God's love right before their eyes. We must make a healthy marriage our responsibility.

To govern our family well, we must take responsibility for training our children. Our future is in their hands. We must train them—not just provide for them. Training requires time. Our children need our time and attention more than they need our money. We must focus on preparing them for the challenges of life. The best way to do this is to spend time with our children. If your schedule is too busy for your children, then your schedule is too busy.

OUR RESPONSIBILITY TO OUR LOCAL CHURCH

Our next responsibility is our involvement in our local church. I do not think that our families and our service in the church need to compete with one another. They are not mutually exclusive. However, some people make the mistake of spending too much time involved at church, causing their family to suffer. We must never allow our family to suffer because we are so busy with responsibilities at church. At the same time, we cannot let our families keep us so busy that we are not involved at church. There is a delicate balance that we must strike with both family and church.

Church and our families were not designed by God to compete with one another. They are to complement one another. The church should build on what you teach your family at home. The time you spend with your family should reinforce what they have heard in church. Family and church work together to raise children—they do not compete with one another.

The key is finding the balance between them. That balance differs for each family. But the truth is that emphasizing one at the expense of the other is wrong. We cannot emphasize family at the expense of church. Then we are not teaching our children about the importance of church. THE MESSAGE Bible in Hebrews 10:24 states:

> *"24Let's see how inventive we can be in encouraging love and helping out, not avoiding worshiping together as some do but spurring each other on, especially as we see the big Day approaching."*

Our children learn the importance of regular church attendance when they see us making it a priority in our family lives.

On the other hand, we cannot keep our families so busy with church activities that they do not do well in school or maintain their responsibilities at home. (It is important that children learn responsibility around the home.)

There is a balance that each family must work diligently to

find. No one can tell you what the proper balance is for your family. But I challenge you to find the balance that optimizes a healthy family with regular involvement in your local church. Both are important!

THERE IS NO FORMULA FOR THE RIGHT BALANCE

So many people want a formula for finding this balance or for living out this balance. Can I tell you the truth? THERE IS NO FORMULA. The only way we will find out what that balance is for our own families is by accepting the fundamental responsibility of developing our own relationship with God. When we give God the time He deserves in our lives, we will hear His voice and understand His direction. He will make things clear to us. I really do not believe that people make a mistake by being too involved with their family or too involved with their church. I think the biggest mistake people make is being too involved with everything else in their lives, so that they cannot hear God's instructions on how to balance their lives.

SO WHERE DOES A CAREER FIT INTO THIS?

Our career fits in around our responsibilities to develop our relationship with God, our family, and our church. I have seen many people make mistakes in this area over the years. They make a decision to advance their career, at the expense of their family, their relationship with their church, and their relationship with God. They get too busy in their career, and they lose the closeness of their personal relationship with God. Then they move away from their church for a promotion. Sometimes without realizing it, they have started pursuing money rather than pursuing God. And in their pursuit of money, they sacrifice other things that are more important than money.

On the other hand, I have had men in my church pass up opportunities for promotions and career changes, because they did not want to separate their family from the church God had called them to. I cannot tell you how important it is to keep career advancement in the right balance with your family and your church. It will pay you great dividends over the long haul, even if in the short term it requires that you pass up a promotion.

OUR RESPONSIBILITY FOR OUR FINANCES

Now let's return once again to our widow woman in the story (2 Kings 4). She is in desperate financial need. She runs to the man of God to help her meet the financial need. As a pastor, I see this all the time. People come to the church all the time when they are in financial trouble. They expect the church to bail them out. Sometimes I wonder if they think the church has changed its name to The Crisis Bank!

I do not believe it is the local church's responsibility to bail people out of their financial crises. And, I *really* do not believe the church is responsible to bail people out when they have mismanaged their financial responsibilities.

The Bible is clear about how we are to handle our money. We should be good stewards of the resources that come into our hands. Proverbs 13:18 (God's Word Translation) states:

"Poverty and shame come to a person who ignores dis-

cipline, but whoever pays attention to constructive criticism will be honored."

Based on this Scripture, we could presume that this man had ignored discipline with his finances. He left his family in poverty and shame.

I really don't think that people just unknowingly fall into debt. I know sometimes unexpected things may happen. We may fall on hard times financially. That could happen to the best of us. But the root cause of many people's debt, I believe, comes from a lack of planning on their part. The lack of planning puts them into a bad financial situation.

FINANCIAL RESPONSIBILITY STARTS WITH DISCIPLINE

Notice again what Proverbs 13:18 states, *"Poverty and shame come to a person who ignores discipline...."*

Do you know what it means to "ignore?" Let me give you an illustration. Let's say you are driving down a road, where the speed limit is posted at 45 miles per hour. You are going 55 miles per hour, when a traffic officer spots you and pulls you over. The first thing he will ask when he approaches is, "Do you know how fast you were going?" You answer, "No, I don't know." Why don't you know? You were not paying attention. You ignored the speed limit sign, and you ignored the speedometer on your car. Now the traffic officer is going to penalize you for your ignorance. He will give you a speeding ticket for ignoring the sign that was right in front of your face.

Ignorance is costly. Too many of us are living in ignorance

when it comes to finances. We live in a time that encourages short-term thinking. We are willing to sabotage our future for a present need or want. We spend recklessly just to satisfy the whim of the moment, to have the latest toy, to show a "prosperous image" to those around us, or to keep pace with our neighbors or relatives or friends. The odd thing about this practice is that those we are trying to keep up with often are in debt for all they have. Let me ask you, why would we want to keep up with someone else's debt?

Disciplining ourselves in financial matters should never be viewed as an adversary, but as an ally. It will help us get to where we want to be. Discipline is simply forcing ourselves to do the uncomfortable things now in order to create the future we desire. It is a systematic method to obtain what we want without getting into unnecessary debt.

Every time we spend money unnecessarily, we steal from our future. Our modern world encourages us to spend today for what we think we need or want, rather than save and invest for the future we want. We make permanent decisions based on temporary circumstances.

JESUS TAUGHT US TO LIVE RESPONSIBLY

Jesus taught us to live responsibly in so many ways. Read Mark 6. In verses 33 to 44, the Bible tells the story of Jesus feeding the 5000 men, along with women and children. The crowd had followed Jesus and the disciples to a deserted place, and they had stayed all day while Jesus taught them. When the day was over, the disciples wanted to send them away to get food. But Jesus fed them all with just five loaves of bread and two fish.

If we are not saving for our future, we cannot expect to have anything when we get there.

Certainly that was miraculous. But let's not miss what happened *after* the miracle. Look closely at verses 42 and 43, where it states: *"[42]So they all ate and were filled. [43]And they took up twelve baskets full of fragments and of the fish."*

After feeding them all, Jesus instructed the disciples to pick up all of the leftovers. Did you get that? Jesus was not casual with God's provision. Even though 5000 men, plus women and children, had been fed, Jesus told the disciples to get the leftovers. Most of us would have ignored the leftovers. We would have just ignored the leftovers, walking off wiping our mouths after we had gotten our stomachs full. "God provided and He will provide again," we might say. That's the way most of us would think. But not Jesus. He was quick to have the disciples pick up the leftovers. He wanted them to be responsible with God's provision.

That is the way we should manage the provision that God gives us. This type of management is not common today. Nor does it come naturally—because we are naturally selfish. We want what we want when we want it. We must learn to manage the resources that God brings into our hands by developing discipline.

THE 10/20/70 RULE

When it comes to financial discipline, I use a simple formula. I call it the 10/20/70 rule. With this formula, I can assure you that you will never be without money. What is the 10/20/70 rule? Let me explain.

Add those three numbers and they equal 100%. The numbers represent 10%, 20%, and 70% of my income. This formula determines what I do with the money that comes into my hands. The first 10% is my tithe, and it belongs to God. The second 20% is what I save and use to make investments. Then I live on the remaining 70%.

Is that a new thought for you? I hope it is! Because if it is, it means I am challenging your thinking. And when your thinking is challenged, you begin to change.

Some of you right now are probably choking at this thought. Your first reaction to this idea may be, "There is no way I could do that! It is impossible!" Now, before you throw this book out the window, give me a chance to explain. I believe that if we are disciplined, we can do amazing things in this life. You may not be able to put this formula to work right this moment, but make it a goal. Work toward it. As you do, you will begin to enjoy the rewards of financial discipline. Those rewards will spur you on to the place where this formula is working for you.

Now let me explain the "10" in the 10/20/70 rule.

THE TITHE

Tithing is pretty unpopular today. It has been reported that fewer than 10% of all born-again believers tithe. That means that over 90% of the church is not tithing. That is amazing to me! I believe Christians do not tithe because they have not been taught why they should.

Tithing is a principle that God established to further the work of His kingdom and to establish a financial covenant between God and His people. When we become kingdom-minded, we will want to put the work of God first. That is what we do when we tithe.

TITHING REFLECTS OUR FEAR OF GOD

First, what is a tithe? The word "tithe" means ten percent. God asks us to put Him first in our finances, by bringing the first ten percent of our income to Him. Deuteronomy 14:22-23 (New Living Translation) gives us an important insight into why God instructs us to tithe. It states:

> *"[22]You must set aside a tithe of your crops—one-tenth of all the crops you harvest each year. [23]Bring this tithe to the place the LORD your God chooses for his name to be honored, and eat it there in his presence. This applies to your tithes of grain, new wine, olive oil, and the firstborn males of your flocks and herds.* ***The purpose of tithing is to teach you always to fear the LORD your God.****"*

God has a specific purpose for tithing. This Scripture reveals that tithing teaches us the fear of God. This is not like the fear of darkness you experienced as a child. No, the fear of God is a reverence, an acknowledgement of who God is. You see, God is the source of everything that you and I have and need. Everything we possess came from Him. Any money we earn resulted from us using our God-given ability to earn that money. What can we do apart from the ability He gives us? Apart from the capacity to think? Apart from the physical strength to work?

The tithe simply acknowledges that *everything* we have came from Him in the first place. When you stop to realize that the whole 100% of what you have came from His hand, is 10% too much to give back to Him? This is GOD we are talking about! Is God not worthy of one dime on every dollar you earn? Think about that…how important is a dime? Can we not believe that God is worthy to receive a dime on every dollar? I believe He is. In fact, I believe that eternity will reveal that He is worth much more than just a dime on every dollar!

THE TITHE IS NOT JUST OLD TESTAMENT LAW

Many people, when they hear teaching on tithing, immediately respond by saying that tithing is an Old Testament law—something that we, as people who live in the New Testament, do not have to bother with. Can I share a Scripture that indicates that such thinking is wrong? Look at Matthew 23:23 in the New Living Translation. It states:

> "[23]*How terrible it will be for you teachers of religious law and you Pharisees. Hypocrites! For you are careful to tithe even the tiniest part of your income, but you ignore the important things of the law—justice, mercy, and faith. You should tithe, yes, but you should not leave undone the more important things.*"

Jesus was talking to the Pharisees about their hypocritical attitudes in this portion of Scripture. He was rebuking them for ignoring matters of the heart, while they were diligent to pay their tithes.

Some people read this and say that Jesus said tithing was

not important, so we do not have to tithe any more. But is that what He really said? I do not think so. Look at His instructions. He told them to do both. He instructed us to be attentive to matters of the heart—matters such as justice, mercy, and truth—AND to tithing. He did not abolish one in favor of the other. He instructed us to do *both*.

Jesus wants us responsible in all areas of life—both matters of the heart and matters of daily life. Tithing is a matter of daily life for a New Testament believer. Jesus did not abolish tithing. He confirmed it, along with the importance of the matters of the heart.

THOSE WHO TITHE ARE BLESSED

I really do not understand why people are so hesitant to trust God with the tithe (the first ten percent). The promise He makes to those who tithe should make us eager to tithe. Look at Malachi 3:10-12. There God instructs us,

> *"10 'Bring all the tithes into the storehouse, That there may be food in My house, And try Me now in this,' Says the LORD of hosts, 'If I will not open for you the windows of heaven and pour out for you such blessing that there will not be room enough to receive it. 11 And I will rebuke the devourer for your sakes, so that he will not destroy the fruit of your ground, nor shall the vine fail to bear fruit for you in the field,' Says the LORD of hosts; 12 'And all nations will call you blessed, For you will be a delightful land,' says the LORD of hosts."*

Some people may think that giving God 10% of their income is a lot to give. But look at what He promises to do for those who bring Him their tithe. He says He will open the windows of heaven and pour out blessings to the point that we will not have room to take it all in. Can you imagine being blessed liked that? God promises that if we will just trust Him with the ten percent, He will give us more than we have room for. But He doesn't stop there.

He goes on to promise that He will rebuke the devourer. I believe that means He will protect what He gives us. In this 21st century life, I believe that means He will bless every area of our life. He promises His protection—materially and spiritually—to those who tithe. And all it takes is that we trust Him by giving Him the first ten percent of our income.

LIFE IS TWO-FOLD: NECESSITIES AND LUXURIES

Once we pay our tithe, we have 90% of our income left. Unfortunately, many people mismanage that money. The reason is because they have confused luxuries and necessities.

Necessities are what we must have to live. They are things like a roof over your head, food to sustain your life, and clothes on your back. These things are every adult's responsibility. Living within your means is the key to not creating unnecessary needs in your life. If you live beyond your means, you are putting yourself behind the eight ball, and that's not a good way to live. Wanting to live the life of luxury is not wrong. But, you have to understand that luxury costs a lot of money, and you may not be able to afford it at this point of your life.

I believe you should be rewarded with the good things in life *after* you have qualified yourself by being responsible. Ecclesiastes 2:24 makes this statement:

"[24]Nothing is better for a man than that he should eat and drink, and that his soul should enjoy good in his labor. This also, I saw, was from the hand of God."

No matter where you are right now financially, it is important that you be willing to start where you are. It is never too late to work toward living by this rule. This whole book is designed to help you do that.

Let me share briefly some thoughts about the 90% of our income left after we tithe.

LEARNING TO SAVE IS A DISCIPLINE TOO!

After we pay our tithe, we should save the next 20% of what we bring home. Again, you may not be able to do this right away, but set a goal. Start saving something today. Saving starts the process of making money work for you rather than always having to work for money. We will talk about this in more detail in Chapter 7 of this book.

CONTROLLING OUR EXPENSES IS THE KEY!

Living on 70% may seem impossible to you right now, but it can be done. Again, it takes discipline. It requires thinking differently about how we spend the money we earn. Controlling our expenses requires a budget. I know that is a scary word for some people, but a budget is really the key to controlling what we spend. It may seem restrictive at first, but once you taste the reward of the discipline of a budget, you will not want to go back to your old, undisciplined ways. (For more on controlling your expenses, see Chapter 6.)

CHANGING THE WAY WE THINK ABOUT LIFE

Now that I have challenged the way you think about being responsible for your life and for the money you make, I want to challenge your thinking about *how* you make your money. Most people go through life expecting to work on a job, day after day, year after year, thinking that is the way we are supposed to live.

I don't buy that. I believe we all have opportunities to increase our income. The problem for most people is that they expect opportunities to chase them down and knock them over. In reality, it doesn't work like that. In most cases, opportunity stands silently in your life waiting for you to recognize it.

We see opportunities when we change the way we think. Most people go through life living as Consumers. Opportunities abound when we learn to think like Producers. What do I mean? I'm glad you asked! Let me challenge your thinking some more in the next chapter!

COMMON SENSE IDEAS

1. Individual responsibility is essential to learning effective money management.
2. Lack of common sense in money management will cause individuals to squander God's blessings.
3. Being spiritual does not equate to being responsible.
4. Preparing for the future today is critical for everyone.
5. Responsibility for the consequences of choices made with money rests with each individual. Decisions on how to spend money earned rests with the earner.
6. What we have in life depends on what we do with what's in our hands.
7. Responsibilities in life must be balanced. Our relationship with God is the top priority.
8. Relationships with spouse and family come right after our relationship with God in our list of priorities.
9. Responsibility to family and the local church should not *compete* with one another; they should complement one another.
10. Not saving for the future negates the expectation to have anything when you get there.
11. Everyone can learn to live by the 10/20/70 rule. Give 10% to God. Save 20% for the future. Live on the remaining 70%.

GOD WANTS
US TO LIVE
LIFE AS
PRODUCERS,
NOT CONSUMERS.

<u>*Chapter 5*</u>

Are You A Consumer or Producer?

COMMON SENSE POINT 2:

We must become Producers rather than just living as Consumers.

We must learn to use the abilities and opportunities God has given us to increase the money we earn in life. We have to change the way we look at life in order to become Producers.

> *"[2]So Elisha said to her, 'What shall I do for you? Tell me, **what do you have in the house?**' And she said, 'Your maidservant has nothing in the house but **a jar of oil.**'*
> *[3] Then he said, '**Go, borrow vessels** from everywhere, from all your neighbors—empty vessels; do not gather just a few. [4]And when you have come in, you shall shut the door behind you and your sons; then pour it into all those vessels, and **set aside the full ones**'" (2 Kings 4:2-3).*

When the widow came to Elisha, she thought her situation was hopeless. From her viewpoint, she could see no way out. She had what I call a "Consumer mentality."

But that is not what Elisha saw. Elisha saw an opportunity for her to change her outlook. Elisha had what I call a "Producer mentality."

Sometimes, opportunity is right in front of us, but because of our limited thinking and shortsightedness, we cannot see it. What did the widow see? Nothing. She saw no way out of the situation because she had the mentality of a Consumer.

What did Elisha see? He saw resources right there in the widow's home. He saw opportunity because he had a Producer mentality.

Look at what Elisha said to the widow in verse 2. *"So Elisha said to her, 'What shall I do for you? Tell me,* ***what do you have in the house?****'"*

I emphasized the question Elisha asked because it is a key to our understanding. Elisha asked her, "What do YOU have in the house?" Elisha wanted her to see that she could do something about the situation. He knew she had the answer, and he wanted her to see it for herself.

I like that about Elisha. He did not want this woman dependent on him. He wanted her to see that she could change the situation for herself. She had what she needed.

IT TAKES WORK AND A CREATIVE MIND TO GET OUT OF DEBT!

Like so many people today, the widow believed she could do NOTHING about her situation. She believed she was a victim and helpless. "I have nothing, man of God. Help me! Give me a promise that God is going to supernaturally reduce my debt, because I have no way out!!"

Today, she might hear preachers promise that God will supernaturally pay off her debt or that God will supernaturally put money in her bank account. To someone like this widow woman, who was so deeply in debt, that kind of hollow promise sounds good. In fact, it can even sound "spiritual" to believe that God would work a miracle to get her out of debt.

But no matter how good it sounds, it is still a lie. I know why people fall for these empty promises. Because it is the easy way out—and our lazy mentality always looks for the easy way out.

The truth is that it takes work to get out of debt. In fact, it takes more work to get out of debt than it does to get into debt. You might not like to hear that, but it is the truth, and if you are willing to accept what I'm saying, it will change your life forever. God wants us to work!

GOD WANTS US TO USE WHAT IS IN OUR HAND TO CHANGE OUR SITUATION

Ecclesiastes 9:10 states: *"Whatever your hand finds to do, do it with your might; for there is no work or device or knowledge or wisdom in the grave where you are going."*

This woman said she had nothing that could change her situation. The pressure of the situation was so great that she could not see her way out. That is what financial pressure does to a lot of people. It blinds them to the opportunities around them.

Financial pressure is one of the worst pressures we can face. It can permeate all aspects of our lives, because everything costs money. When we are under financial pressure, we see everything differently. It tends to limit our vision.

Still, God always knows what is available to us. If we will

listen to Him, God will show us what is available to change the situations we face.

Moses had a rod in his hand, but he did not see it as anything of value until God opened his eyes (Exodus 4). God told Joshua to stretch out his hand with a spear toward the city of Ai (Joshua 8:18). Joshua was not impressed with the spear, until God showed him what He could do with it. When he stretched out his hand with the spear, God delivered the city of Ai into his hands.

Elijah asked the widow of Zarephath what was in her hand. She said she only had a handful of flour (1 Kings 17:11-12). She did not see the provision in her hand, either. But when she used what was in her hand, God blessed her.

The disciples said they only had five loaves and two fish—not enough to feed a crowd of 5,000 (see Mark 6:33-44). But Jesus saw enough to feed 5,000 and still have food left over.

The point here is that God always can use something we have in our hand—if we believe it and are willing to do the work. But, God won't move until we are willing to use what's in our hands.

I want you to read the following poem. It is a great example of what can happen to something when it's in the hands of a person who can see the value of it. It is not what is in your hand that matters, but rather what you do with what is in your hand that makes all the difference.

A basketball in my hands is worth about $19.
A basketball in Michael Jordan's hands is worth about $33 million.
It all depends on whose hands it's in...

A baseball in my hands is worth about $6.
A baseball in Mark McGuire's hands is worth about $19 million.
It depends on whose hands it's in...

A golf club is almost useless in my hands.
A golf club in Tiger Woods' hands can win 4 Major Golf Championships.
It depends on whose hands it's in...

A rod in my hands will keep away a wild animal.
A rod in Moses' hands will part the mighty sea.
It depends on whose hands it's in...

A slingshot in my hands is a toy.
A slingshot in David's hands is a mighty weapon.
It depends on whose hands it's in...

Two fish and five loaves in my hands is a couple of fish sandwiches.
Two fish and fives loaves in Jesus' hands will feed thousands.
It depends on whose hands they're in...

Nails in my hands might produce a birdhouse.
Nails in Christ Jesus' hands will produce salvation for the entire world.
It depends on whose hands they're in...

As you see now, it depends on whose hands it's in...

So put your concerns, your worries, your fears, your hopes, your dreams, your families, and your relationships in God's hands because...
It depends on whose hands they're in.

Used by permission: Pastor Paul Ciniraj
of Salem Voice, Kottayam, Kerala, India

We can look at all these examples and say: "That doesn't apply to us. They were all special—what was in their hand became worth a lot of money."

Stop and think. The basketball in Michael Jordan's hands started with a value of $19. He was nothing special until he began to use what was in his hand. It's the same with Mark McGuire or Tiger Woods, or anyone else you can name. They started with something that seemed insignificant, but they started with what was in their hands. And their willingness to work hard brought them great reward.

What is in your hand?

ELISHA INSTRUCTED THE WIDOW TO START WITH WHAT WAS IN HER HAND

Look at the woman in our story again. She told Elisha she had nothing, except a jar of oil. She saw only a little jar of oil, but Elisha saw much more. Elisha saw an opportunity. Elisha knew she had something in her hand. It did not seem like much to the woman. It may not have seemed like much to Elisha, but it was something.

The difference between Elisha and the woman is that Elisha saw that something could be done. And he gave the woman the instructions she needed. Look at what he said to her in verse 3:

> "[3]*Then he said, '**Go, borrow vessels** from everywhere, from all your neighbors—empty vessels; do not gather just a few.* [4]*And when you have come in, you shall shut the door behind you and your sons; then pour it into all those vessels, and **set aside the full ones.**'"*

GOD WANTS US TO WORK!

When we are looking for a quick fix, God gives us something else. He will take us through a process, rather than give us a quick fix. That is what He did with this woman through Elisha's instructions to her.

What did Elisha tell her to do? He told her to go to work! WHAT? HE TOLD HER TO GO TO WORK?

Yes, that is exactly what he told her to do. He told her to go to work—to go borrow vessels! He did not make it easy on her. He did not tell her to go to just one place to borrow one or two vessels. He told her to go everywhere and every place to borrow vessels. He told her to borrow not just a few but many of them.

If that is not work, I don't know what it is. Can you imagine going everywhere to borrow vessels? That took time and effort. She could not just go home and sit down and pray for God to do something to reduce her debt. She had to go to work. She had to put out some effort. She had to go borrow the vessels. She had to get involved in the situation rather than just sit and wait for God to do something.

When she had collected all the vessels, she still had more

work to do. She had to start with the little she had and use it. She could not just sit and wait for God to move. She had to get involved in the process. She started with nothing and did something.

You know what she did? She set up an assembly line in her home. And she got her sons involved in the production. She did not allow them to sit and watch, doing nothing about the problem. She poured oil, and they brought the vessels. They set aside the vessels once they were full. They were all working out the solution together.

GOD ADDED HIS "SUPER" AFTER THEY HAD DONE THEIR "NATURAL"

Now, did a miracle occur here? Yes, it did. No one, using only their own abilities, could fill many vessels with oil from just one little jar. So, God did intervene in the natural. But if we focus only on the miracle, we miss out on a valuable practical application.

God did the "super," but she had to do the "natural." She had to do her part; otherwise, there would have not been enough provision for the need. Let me say this: nothing leaves heaven until something happens on earth. This woman's willingness to do her part permitted God to do His part.

What if she had only gotten a couple vessels from her neighbors? The jar of oil would have stopped after she filled only a few vessels. She would have missed the provision if she had been careless or lazy in her work. The oil kept multiplying because they continued to provide vessels to be filled.

GOD WANTED THE WIDOW TO BECOME A PRODUCER IN LIFE

What happened after they had filled all the vessels? She had obeyed Elisha's first instruction. She had borrowed the vessels and had filled them all with oil. When she had finished doing that, she had a home full of vessels—all filled with oil. But she still did not see what she had. She just saw a home full of oil.

So what did she do? Did she just sit down and wait for God to perform another miracle? Did God just "supernaturally" pay off their debt? NO! She went back to the man of God for another instruction. Read verse 7 of 2 Kings 4. It states:

> *"7 Then she came and told the man of God. And he said, '**Go, sell the oil and pay your debt**; and you and your sons live on the rest.'"*

I can almost hear this widow woman's response: "What, man of God? What did you say? Go sell it? Did I hear you right? Wait a minute! I am a housewife! I am a mother! I am not a salesperson! I don't know how to do that!"

Do you see the point I am trying to make? So many times opportunities are right in front of us, but we do not see them because we are looking at life from the wrong perspective.

Too many preachers today are telling people to just believe God for a miracle—supernatural debt reduction! But that is NOT what God did for this woman. What God gave her was an opportunity! He blessed her with an economic opportunity. He changed her life from being a Consumer to being a Producer. And He wants to do the same for you.

ARE YOU A CONSUMER OR A PRODUCER?

God's instructions, through Elisha, helped this woman move from being a Consumer to becoming a Producer. God wants to do the same thing with you. There are things you are not seeing in your life today, and it could be costing you dearly. The way we view life causes us to be a Consumer or a Producer.

How many of us are sitting on some kind of talent that God deposited inside us from conception, yet we do not recognize it? Someone once said that the richest place on the planet is the cemetery. I agree with that! Too many people die with their dreams buried inside them.

I love to say it this way: *Your wealth is inside you!* Your wealth is not the money in your pocket. It is your ability to be creative, to produce something, and then exchange it for money.

One of my favorite verses of Scripture is Jeremiah 1:5 (NKJV), which states:

> *"5Before I formed you in the womb I knew you; before you were born I sanctified you; I ordained you a prophet to the nations."*

You are pre-programmed by God to succeed in what He has created you to do. All that you need to do to succeed in this life is to discover what God has placed in you. Discover the wealth He has put inside you! Your wealth is not in the hands of an employer, but in your ability to produce in life.

You cannot celebrate something if you do not understand its purpose. We must understand the purpose of the abilities inside us. If we do not understand that God has given us gifts to develop and use, we will not recognize them. In fact, we can take the abilities in us for granted and miss the purpose for which God has given them. When we do not use the abilities and the talents that God has given us, then we miss the blessings that He has planned for us.

Whatever you do not recognize in you will go uncelebrated.

Not too long ago, people who received the Nobel Peace Prize were unheard of by the world community. Now, they are on center stage worldwide. Why? Because their talents are now being recognized and celebrated. The talents of the Nobel Peace Prize recipients are being used to solve various kinds of problems that impact or help humanity. They are now being rewarded with international recognition.

Whatever abilities you don't recognize in your life, you become unqualified to keep. Remember the man who had the one talent (Matthew 25:14-28)? In his mind, he thought his talent had no value, so he never used it to its full capability. Guess what? He eventually lost it. That can happen to us also. If we do not appreciate the value of the abilities and talents we have, we will end up losing them.

WHAT YOU HAVE IN YOUR HAND WILL DETERMINE YOUR ECONOMIC STATUS IN LIFE

Are you *seeing* what is in your hand? What you have can take many forms. For some, it is physical ability. For others, it is physical beauty. Others have creative minds or artistic skills or acting ability or negotiating skills or speaking ability or organizational skills. Everybody has something in them that has the potential to prosper them in life. The question is whether we recognize it, understand its purpose, celebrate it and put it to work.

Anything uncelebrated becomes unrewarded.

WHAT IS A CONSUMER?

People who have a Consumer mentality do not see their gifts or their opportunities to prosper. They see the world as a place to spend money, rather than a place to produce and increase their wealth.

A Consumer is someone who is a waster, someone who absorbs everything in sight. In other words, everything stops in the hands of a Consumer. A Consumer is an entrance only, never an exit. Consumers are like the Dead Sea in Israel. A lot of water flows into the Dead Sea, but because it has no exit, everything that enters dies there.

If you are a Consumer, spending all that comes into your life, don't be surprised when your creditors choose the lifestyle you will live.

A Consumer mentality keeps us from seeing our abilities

and talents. Consumers discount the value of what they have available. They miss the value of the abilities or talents they have or the opportunities presented to them.

Proverbs 13:23 (New Century Version) states:

"[23]A poor man's field might have plenty of food. But unfair people steal it from him." This Scripture always provokes me to challenge people who are not making it financially to begin to look within themselves, instead of waiting for some kind of false hope from others.

You see, friends, what you fail to see in yourself, you will end up purchasing from someone else. Proverbs 13:4 states: *"The soul of a lazy man (or we can say a Consumer) desires, and has nothing; But the soul of the diligent shall be made rich."*

Consumers are not diligent in discovering what is in them and putting it to work.

CONSUMERS HAVE A "BOX MENTALITY"

I believe people are Consumers because of a "box mentality" in life. They allow society to box them into thinking no room exists for their creative ideas, so they accept a "box mentality."

From the day we came into this world until the day we die, people will try to put us into boxes. Think about this: when you were born, the first thing your parents did was put you into a crib. In their mind, it was a place of safety. But in reality, it was the start of the "box mentality" that has followed you all your life.

From the "crib box," you went into the "school box," where you were told to color between the lines, write between the lines, and stay in line. They made you sit at a box—they called it a desk.

Anything uncelebrated will eventually exit your life.

In school, they taught us to stay in our "boxes."

After the "school box" came the "work box." You sit in a box called a cubicle or an office. And, you are paid a salary determined by someone else. I call that a "salary box," because you are told how much you are worth.

After years of being confined to the "work box," society demands that you go into the "retirement box." They expect you to sit in that box and not do much, wasting all the experience that you have accumulated over the years. And there you wait to die.

And when you die, guess what? It is the saddest thing of all. You guessed it! You end up six feet under ground in your "final box"—a casket.

I rebel against the "box mentality." God never designed us to live with a "box mentality."

CONSUMERS ARE THE CUSTOMERS OF PRODUCERS

Consumers settle for being the customers of Producers. Have you ever noticed that everything you own was designed by somebody else? You are the Producer's customer. And in some cases, you have become their advertisement.

Here is a good example. When you go to the store, do you

always buy a brand-name? If you do, you have just become an advertisement for the Producer of that product. I don't care if you wear brand names. But do it because you want to wear it, not just because it is the popular thing to do. Don't allow a Consumer mentality to reduce you to becoming someone else's advertisement.

The Characteristics of a Consumer Mentality

- *They let fear dictate and paralyze their movement in life.*
- *They have more faith in what they cannot do than in what they can do.*
- *They love to be entertained instead of being productive in life.*
- *They have more pleasure in spending their earnings than saving them.*
- *They believe that the future is now, so they sabotage their future for their present need.*
- *They are always borrowing from the future.*
- *They are out of control with their spending because they are driven by need.*

GOD CREATED YOU TO BE A PRODUCER, NOT JUST A CONSUMER!

I always like to look at Genesis 1:26-28 for the pattern that God wants us to follow. You see, the first two chapters of Genesis reveal God's plans for this world. Genesis 1 and 2 are accounts of life on earth before sin entered. These two chapters record God's ideal plan for us. And, I believe what God said to us in the Garden of Eden is still His will for us today in the 21st century.

Look at what God said in verses 26-31:

> "[26]*Then God said, 'Let Us make man in Our image, according to Our likeness; let them have dominion over the fish of the sea, over the birds of the air, and over the cattle, over all the earth and over every creeping thing that creeps on the earth.'* [27]*So God created man in His own image; in the image of God He created him; male and female He created them.* [28]*Then God blessed them, and God said to them, '**Be fruitful and multiply**; fill the earth and **subdue** it; **have dominion** over the fish of the sea, over the birds of the air, and over every living thing that moves on the earth.'* [29]*And God said, 'See, I have given you every herb that yields seed which is on the face of all the earth, and every tree whose fruit yields seed; to you it shall be for food.* [30]*Also, to every beast of the earth, to every bird of the air, and to everything that creeps on the earth, in which there is life, I have given every green herb for food'; and it was so.* [31]*Then God saw everything that He had made, and indeed it was very good. So the evening and the morning were the sixth day."*

Notice that God did not say: "Adam, sit back and chill out. I have made all of this for you to be lazy, so just sit around and enjoy it." NO! God told Adam to work, to be productive, to use everything that God had made to be fruitful. God *could* have made it so that we could just sit and be lazy, but that is not what He did. The only miracle that Adam received from God was his physical body. For everything else, Adam used the abilities and talents God had given him to produce something.

When God said to Adam, "Be blessed," He was saying, "I empowered you to be what I designed you to be." God put everything we need on the inside of us. We just need to discover and release what God has put in us. The way we do that is to be faithful in doing what our hand finds to do. We cannot discover what God has put into us by sitting idle and doing nothing.

PRODUCERS HAVE DISCOVERED WHAT GOD PLACED INSIDE THEM

God wants all of us to be Producers of some kind. That is why He gave us talents and abilities. Look at what the Bible states in Proverbs 12:24 in The Living Bible:

> *"[24]Work hard and become a leader; be lazy (or a Consumer) and never succeed."*

His will for us has not changed! God wants us to be productive in life. Yet, so many people still waste their time and talents being Consumers rather than being Producers.

Producers think differently from Consumers. Producers look at life through a different lens than Consumers. Producers see what Consumers do not see. And Producers are able to capitalize on what they see. Producers look for creative solutions. They seek out new and better ways of solving problems. Then they are rewarded for solving the problem. What is the reward they receive? MONEY and INFLUENCE!

That is why developing the mentality of a Producer is critical to keeping the creditors from coming to your home. With the mentality of a Producer, you can use your God-given abilities to generate an income that will allow you to detemine your lifestyle. Not only will you be able to pay your bills, you will be able to release opportunities for other people. A Producer actually provides opportunities for other people!

Characteristics of Producers

- *They understand their value in life.*
- *They discover what they can do and are not afraid to step out and do it.*
- *They sacrifice and invest time in developing their abilities.*
- *They allow sacrifice to teach them what it takes to make it.*
- *They build wealth for their future.*
- *They are those who discover and use the laws that govern success.*
- *They never sit on first base, when there are other bases to cover in life.*

Producers understand that when their gifts and abilities are developed and utilized through their life's work, they grow in confidence and success.

Consumers may think that Producers are just more fortunate people. Consumers assume that Producers have some special calling or gifting that allows them to succeed in life. I do not believe that. Producers are just willing to do things that Consumers are not willing to do—or are not disciplined enough to do. Producers do what Consumers only think about doing.

GOD CHALLENGED THE WIDOW WOMAN TO BECOME A PRODUCER

The capital to start a business was already in the woman's home, awaiting her recognition of it. She did not see what she had. She only saw a jar of oil. She did not see the potential in the oil. She only saw it as something she could consume, not something she could use. In her Consumer thinking, the jar of oil was not enough to do anything for her situation. When you change your way of thinking from that of a Consumer to that of a Producer, amazing things begin to happen. You start to see opportunities you did not see before. You start to work to make those opportunities come to pass. You start to increase your income. You start to increase your financial value in life. You start to add to your bank account, rather than subtracting from it.

It literally pays to think differently, because when you think differently, you position yourself to get different results. When you think like a Producer, you can dramatically increase the income in your life. When you increase your income, you are in a better position to keep the creditors from coming to your home.

But, simply increasing your income is not enough, if you are not willing to control your spending. Remember when I talked about learning to live on 70% of your income? That can happen, when we learn to control our spending. Now let's take some time in the next chapter for some practical advice on controlling your spending. That is the third point we want to discuss in keeping the creditors from coming to your home.

COMMON SENSE IDEAS

1. God wants us to use what is in our hand to change our situation. What is in your hand?

2. When looking for a quick fix, God gives us a process.

3. God wants us to live life as Producers, not Consumers.

4. Producers use the resources they have to change their situation in life.

5. Producers understand their value in life. Producers build wealth for their future.

6. Wealth is within each of us. God pre-programmed each person to succeed with the abilities He provided us.

7. Wealth is not in the hands of your employer, but in your ability to produce in life.

8. A Consumer mentality keeps individuals from seeing their abilities and talents.

9. Consumers have a "box mentality."

10. Consumers allow fear to paralyze them in life.

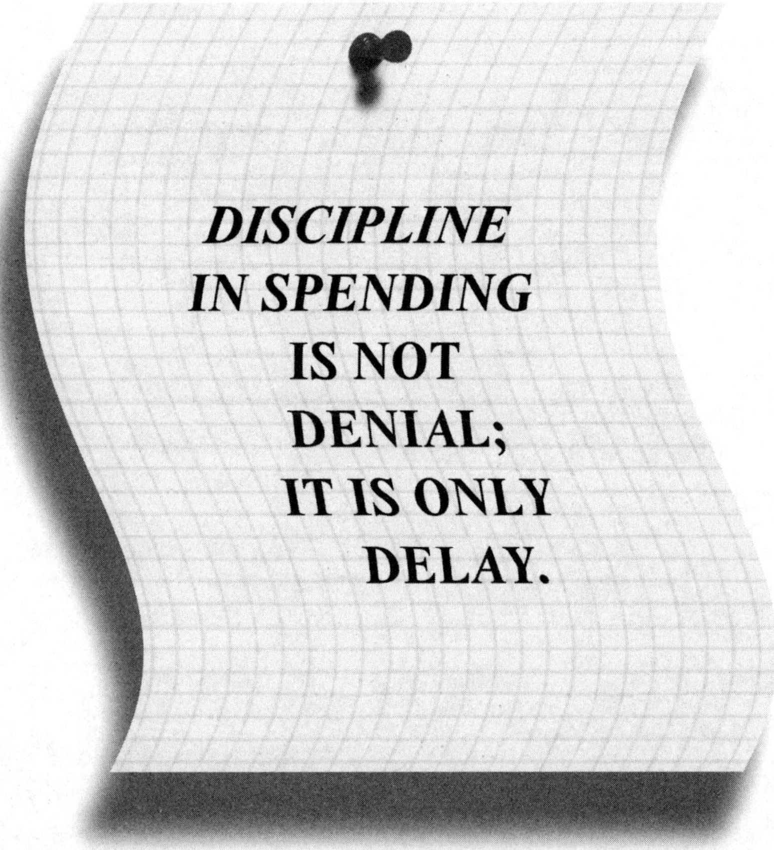
DISCIPLINE
IN SPENDING
IS NOT
DENIAL;
IT IS ONLY
DELAY.

Chapter 6

Common Sense Money Management

COMMON SENSE POINT 3:

We must manage the money we make by controlling our spending as our income rises.

We must discipline our spending to preserve our future. We *can* live on less than we think. We must focus on paying off our debts. We must learn to manage the seasons in life.

> *“[7]Then she came and told the man of God. And he said, ‘**Go, sell the oil and pay your debt**; and you and your sons live on the rest’” (2 Kings 4:7).*

In the previous chapter, we talked about increasing our income by becoming a Producer in life. But does just increasing our income assure that we can keep the creditors from coming to our home? Many people think so. They think their only problem is not having enough money. They reason that if they only had more money, all their problems would be solved.

That is not necessarily true. No matter how big our

income, if we do not learn how to manage the money we earn, we will spend all we make and remain in debt—or go even further into debt.

Many people just do not understand that simple thinking. When they start to make more money, they start to spend more money. They buy the things they could not buy when they were making less money. They go places they could not go. Instead of working their way *out of debt,* they just spend more money. They still find themselves in financial difficulties. So, they think they just need even more money—and the cycle begins again.

If that is the way you function, this section is just for you. It takes more than just making more money to get out of debt. It requires discipline and a new mindset.

MONEY MANAGEMENT IS NOT THAT COMPLEX!

I wrote this book because I want to provide people with some common-sense ways to succeed in the area of finances. I don't want people to suffer because they mismanage their money. Money management is not that complex. What we must do is spend less than we make. The creditors will NEVER come to our home, if we just do that!

But, too many believers are irresponsible with their money. And then they try to "spiritualize" it.

What do I mean by that? I am referring to people who spend more than they earn and then say, "The devil is attacking my finances." Or they spend all they earn each month, living paycheck to paycheck. Then, when an expensive repair is needed on their vehicle, they scream, "The devil is attacking my finances."

I am sorry, ladies and gentlemen. If you are living like that, it is not because the devil is attacking your finances. It is because you are a poor manager of your money! The devil gets blamed for things he did not have anything to do with. It is not the devil's fault if we do not manage our money well. It is not the devil's fault if we spend more than we make each month. It is not the devil's fault if our washing machine wears out after 15 years of washing three loads of clothes four times a week! Let's quit blaming the devil and accept some responsibility for learning how to manage money.

Too many people think they can spend their money on anything they want, expecting God to bail them out of any financial difficulty that may result. They spend irresponsibly, live without a budget, and buy on impulse. Then when reality hits, they think they can just run to God and ask for a financial miracle. I do not believe that God will bless that type of irresponsibility.

I believe in the "Gospel of responsibility." God wants us to live responsible lives—even in our finances. So many people mail their brains when they get saved. The Bible tells us to *renew* our minds (Romans 12:2). It does not tell us to *remove* our minds.

GOD'S INSTRUCTIONS ON MANAGING MONEY

Let's look at our story again. God wanted this woman to learn how to manage money. He gave her some very simple instructions through Elisha.

Look at His last instructions to this woman in 2 Kings 4:7.

Elisha states: *"Go, **sell the oil** and **pay your debt**; and you and your sons **live on the rest.**"*

Elisha gave the woman three very important, *common-sense* instructions. These were:

1. ***Sell the oil!***
   In other words, "Get to work and earn some money." We talked about that in the last chapter. God wants us to be Producers and not only Consumers.
2. ***Pay your debt!***
   This doesn't need much explanation. Pay off the debt you have accumulated. Make it a priority to PAY the debt—not believe God to "supernaturally reduce" your debt.
3. ***Live on the rest!***
   In other words, "Now that you have an income and your debts are paid, manage what you have. Control your spending and build wealth." The problem with too many people who need to get out of debt is that they have no vision for having wealth. (We will talk about that in the next chapter.)

> ***An instruction is always God's way of helping you solve your problems. God wants you to learn something new.***

It is important for us to understand these common-sense principles so we can keep the creditors from coming to our home. Let me lay out some common sense concepts designed to keep the creditors from coming to your home.

The more problems we solve, the more money we make.

OUR INCOME is the amount of money we make. It is what we get in exchange for the problems we solve on a regular basis.

Generally, we think that people who make a lot of money (or have a BIG income) are RICH. But that is not always true. People can make a lot of money, but if they spend it all every month, they are no better off than someone with a much smaller income who spent it all. THEY ARE BOTH BROKE AT THE END OF THE MONTH!

RICH is a result of spending less than we make each month and then doing something constructive with the money we have left. RICH does NOT mean just having a BIG income. If we spend less than we make, and then manage well what we have left over, each of us can begin to build wealth.

We all have read stories about people who never make big salaries during their lives, but still die multi-millionaires. We've also read about big-name athletes or Hollywood stars who make HUGE incomes during their lifetime, but wind up penniless. How can that happen? It all comes down to managing the money that we make. And that starts with spending less than what we make.

WEALTH AND INCOME ARE NOT THE SAME!

Proverbs 22:7 states: *"The rich rules over the poor, and*

Your income is what you earn; wealth is what you are worth.

the borrower is servant to the lender."

Wealth and income are not the same and, if you don't know the difference, the rich will continue to rule over you.

I talk to so many people who are up to their necks in debt, and they don't know how they got there. I always tell people that when you don't pay attention to the details in your life, you will pay someone to fix them for you. You can't live your life spending money like there is no tomorrow. That way of thinking is irresponsible. When you think like that, you can't blame anyone but yourself for being in unnecessary debt. People who have assets are the ones who are in control in today's society.

Proverbs 13:11 in the New Living Translation states: "[11]*Wealth from get-rich-quick schemes quickly disappears; wealth from hard work grows."*

When we spend less than we make each month, extra money will be available at the end of each month. You can use this extra money to build for the future. We build wealth by acquiring assets that work for us; such assets actually make money for us. As we continue to have extra money each month, we can acquire additional assets that will build more and more wealth. Our assets will earn more and more money for us. But, it all starts by **learn-**

ing to manage our expenses so we spend less than we make each month.

Expenses < Income = Opportunity to Build Wealth

Each of us can learn to live this way. It just takes some understanding and discipline.

MOST PEOPLE LIVE IN A MIRAGE OF WEALTH

However, some people have lived so long in what I call "maintenance mode" that it is hard for them to envision living any other way. What do I mean by that? When we spend everything we earn, we are in maintenance mode. We simply stay in the same place financially, month after month and year after year. We make money today, and we spend it all tomorrow. We are living by impulse rather than by design. We are not building wealth. We are not preparing for the future. We do not advance. We do not improve our position.

Income = Expenses = Maintenance Mode

Let me go a bit further. If you are living in maintenance mode, you are living in a mirage of wealth. Your spending will eventually catch up with you. Financial reality will hit—and it will hit hard.

Maintenance Mode + An Unexpected Expense = Debt

In maintenance mode, one unexpected bill will cause us to go into debt. Think about it! Because we have spent all of our income, we have no extra money to pay unexpected expenses. So when an unexpected expense hits (like a car breaking down, or an appliance needing replacement, or a child needing braces), we have to borrow money to pay for it. We go into debt. And for most people, the delicate balance of maintenance mode is disrupted for months....and maybe even years.

MAINTENANCE MODE IS THE DOORWAY TO MOUNTING DEBT

When the balance of living in maintenance mode is disrupted by one unexpected expense, many people turn to credit cards to solve the problem. They think they can charge just this one unexpected expense on their credit card. They somehow believe they will be able to pay that credit card bill when it comes.

Do you see the flaw in that thinking? If they are in maintenance mode, THERE IS NO EXTRA MONEY. When the credit card bill comes at the end of next month, there will be nothing extra to pay the bill. So they put something else on the credit card. And the cycle begins. Debt starts to pile up, and there seems to be no way to break the cycle. Creditors start calling, not because of the lack of income, but because of the lack of good management. They were living in maintenance mode—the doorway to debt.

Most people are deceived into thinking they can break this cycle easily, once it starts. They think they just have to work harder or make more money. The reality is that this cycle is not easily broken. That is why credit-card debt in this country keeps rising.

Answer the following questions to determine if you are in trouble with your credit-card debt:

- Do you pay only the minimum payment most months?
- Are you maxed out on any of your cards?
- Do you find yourself buying things on credit cards, thinking you will be able to pay them off at the end of the month, and then find you do not have the money to pay off the whole bill?
- Do you use your credit cards to make purchases for things like groceries or clothes or gasoline because you do not have the cash to pay for them?
- Are you concerned that people close to you will find out what your real financial situation is?

If you answer "yes" to any or all of these questions, you are in financial trouble already. It is time to stop playing games with your finances and get serious about paying off your debt.

I also want to warn people who think that low interest rates—or no interest rates—on credit cards will keep them out of financial trouble. To me, this is flawed thinking. If you put money on ANY credit card because you cannot pay the bill with cash, you have spent more than you have made. It doesn't make any difference that the interest rate is low. The truth is, you are spending more than you make each month—and you are in financial trouble.

WE HAVE TO THINK DIFFERENTLY TO GET OUT OF DEBT!

We have to change our thinking in order to get out of debt or to get out of maintenance mode. We have to change our thinking before we are able to build wealth. It starts by learning to manage our expenses. But we will never learn to manage our expenses without managing the way we think. Most people who cannot manage their expenses cannot manage their impulses. Impulse buying starts with impulse thinking.

It is sad to see people who are already in debt continue to sabotage their future for a present need—buying something with no lasting value. I believe we sometimes allow the pressures of this materialistic society to deceive us into thinking that just because something is on sale, we have to purchase it, even when we know we are not in a position to do so.

If you are tempted to buy something just because it is on sale, ask yourself, "Will this purchase help me in my quest to get out of debt?" If there is any doubt in your mind about whether it will help you, you don't need to buy it. Just walk away. Doing that develops discipline. You will feel better about yourself and you will begin to develop the confidence that you can get out of debt.

DISCIPLINE IN SPENDING WILL BRING FINANCIAL FREEDOM

Do you know that a lack of discipline will always disqualify you from any endeavor you attempt in life? Hebrews 12:11 from the New International Version states:

> *"No discipline seems pleasant at the time, but painful. Later on, however, it produces a harvest of righteousness and peace for those who have been trained by it."*

Discipline in financial matters should never be viewed as an adversary, but as an ally to get you where you want to be. Financial discipline is simply forcing yourself to do the uncomfortable thing in the present in order to create the future you desire. It is a systematic method of obtaining what you want, without getting into unnecessary debt.

If you don't prepare for your future, the future will not be prepared for you.

Many people look at discipline in finances as restrictive. Although they know it is the right thing to do, they believe they are "depriving" themselves of things they want. In order to embrace discipline in finances, you have to change that thinking. Discipline in finances is not *denial;* it is only *delay.* Denial means we will *never* have it. Delay means we will have it *at the right time.* Discipline is the foundation for having what we really want. Discipline in finances today assures us that we can have what we want in the future. A lack of discipline today assures us that we *will never* have what we want in the future.

Some may say, "But who knows if I am going to be around for the future? Why can't I just have what I want now?" That thinking is a sure road to financial disaster. As I always say, "If you do not die today, you will wake up tomorrow." In other words, the future does come. And in order to be prepared for it, we must discipline ourselves today.

Let me give you an example from my own personal life. I like to go to Starbucks, the coffee shop that is now spreading around the world. I order the same drink each day. In fact, the associates at this local Starbucks know me so well that they start to make my beverage when they see me walking toward the store. I order a Venti (which means LARGE), soy chai tea latte. Do you know how much that costs? What's my point in this? I was recently thinking about how much money I spend on that one daily drink throughout an entire year. I was amazed to figure out I spend about $1,400 per year at Starbucks for this one daily drink. That was somewhat of a surprise to me. It is not that I cannot afford it—it is just that I had never stopped to consider what it was costing me!

I bet there are things like that in your life: something you are spending money on regularly without realizing how much it is costing you overall. If you are trying to get out of debt, you must consider these types of things. Several things are probably costing you money that you don't need to spend when you are in debt.

Now don't take me wrong! I am not against Starbucks, but I am all for getting out of debt. If you are battling with debt, you can live without these types of things for a while. Look at your phone bill or your cell-phone bill or your cable subscription or your magazine subscriptions, or even the number of times and the places you eat out. We can cut back in many areas. We just have to be willing to look for them!

COMMON SENSE STEPS TO GETTING OUT OF DEBT

I want to share some practical ideas on how you can learn to control your spending and get out of debt. Please do not mistake this section as a book on financial advice. I am not a financial advisor. I am a pastor who wants to help people. What I am going to present here are common-sense things you can do.

Here is a simple process you can follow to get out of debt:

1. Find out how much you owe.
2. Set up a budget.
3. Focus on paying off the debt.
4. Get a vision for building wealth.

As I walk through these practical steps, you may find yourself needing the help of an expert in financial advice. Go to someone you trust in this field. If you do not know one yourself (someone who is credible and really knows what he or she is talking about), ask people you know to recommend someone. People who have started to accumulate wealth may be able to direct you to someone. (Now don't go to someone who just *looks wealthy.* Again, just because someone has a lot of "stuff" does not mean they know how to manage money. You need to find someone who really knows how to manage money.) Don't let your pride get in the way when it comes to asking for help. This is your future we are talking about. Ask someone you can trust to help you.

<u>Step 1: Find out how much you owe</u>

I am amazed by people who do not know how much debt they actually have. They come to the church and ask for help with their finances. What they want is a handout. *They* do not see it that way, but it is the truth. They just think they need help for the moment. When I find out about their situation, I realize what they really need is better financial management.

How do I know that? Because when I start to question them, I find out they do not know how they got into financial trouble, and they do not know how much they really owe. They may say it was a one-time occurrence, but in reality, they have been living in maintenance mode, and they have no plan for how to get out of maintenance mode. I would not be helping them if I gave them a handout. I would be enabling their poor financial habits for one more month. The best way for me to help these people is to teach them, not just bail them out with more money.

You have to learn to pay attention to the little things in order to manage your money. You have to know what you owe. Take the time to sit down and figure it out. I know that can be a challenge emotionally. It can be scary. But if you don't find out how much you owe, you will never be able to figure out a way to pay it off.

Include all your debts: credit cards, car payments, house payments, loans for other recreational vehicles, and any other outstanding loans (school loans, etc). Account for ALL the money you owe. It may be hard to look at that number—it may even seem overwhelming, but it is a critical number to know.

By figuring out how much you owe, you at least give yourself a chance to start paying it off. This first step is critical to the next step.

Step 2: Set up a budget

Once you understand how much you owe, you can begin to plan how to pay it off. That is where your budget comes in. A budget is a plan. It is a plan for your finances. If you have no plan, then you will spend on anything that comes along. A budget helps you make informed decisions about what you do with your money.

A budget keeps us disciplined. Discipline in financial matters always starts with a budget. A budget simply determines how we will manage our income and our outgo. If you do not know what you have coming in and going out, how can you manage your resources responsibly?

Start your budget with what you earn—your income. How much money do you have coming in? What you bring in determines your limits. You have to operate on less than what you bring in. You cannot pay off your debt without spending less than what you make. Put your total monthly income down first.

Then, make a list of all your monthly expenses. Some people do not know all that they spend every month. If you don't, get out a piece of paper TODAY, and start making a list of every penny that you spend. Write it down. This may seem hard to do, but this is where discipline starts. Make categories for your household, if you want. Make sure those categories work for your family.

I have included a section that can help you track your expenses. It is not the final word on how to categorize your expenses, but it can be a place to start.

Checklist for Monthly Expenses

- ☐ **Tithes and offerings:** what money do you give to advance the kingdom of God every month?
- ☐ **Housing**: including your rent or mortgage, and all the utility payments, and a monthly allotment for your insurance. Also include all the items you buy to maintain your home: cleaning supplies, appliances, furnishings, etc.
- ☐ **Food:** what you buy at the grocery store. Include all the little items you buy, also. That bottle of pop or water, or the bag of chips, etc.

- ☐ **Transportation**: your car payment, the gas, a monthly allotment for insurance and repairs. Or maybe your transportation is bus or taxi or train. Account for all of it. Include tolls, too.
- ☐ **Health care**: what medical expenses do you have each month? Include in this category such other related items like haircuts, cosmetics, nail care, etc.
- ☐ **Clothing**: This number may be a little bit harder to figure out, because most of us do not buy clothing every day or every week. We buy clothes over time, so it is harder to determine what we spend on that. But with some work, you can do it.
- ☐ **School expenses**: what are the things your children need for school? Things like paper, pencils, backpacks, activities, or athletics and their clothes.
- ☐ **Entertainment**: include everything outside of the other categories—the money you spend at restaurants or coffee shops, the movies you go to or rent, the electronics equipment you buy, the cell phone you carry, the cable bill, the internet bill, the sports in which you participate, the health club dues or fees, the tanning salons, magazine subscriptions, newspaper subscriptions, etc.
- ☐ **Your monthly debt payments:** account for the minimum payments you have to make each month.

If you have a hard time coming up with these numbers, look at your checkbook or your bank statement. You must also keep all of your receipts. Then sit down and make a list of what you bought and how much it cost.

Does this sound like work? Guess what? It is. No matter what you think, it will take some serious work to get out of debt. Finding out how much you spend is critical.

Once you have figured out your monthly expenses, compare that number to what you earn each month. The comparison will determine how big the problem really is. It will also determine how much of an adjustment you will have to make to get out of debt.

When you know how much more you are spending each month than you are bringing home, then you can focus on cutting out what you don't need. How you look at this process is critical. If you see this as *denial*, you will most likely fail. If you see this as *delay*, then you will succeed in this difficult process. Remember, if you do not prepare for your future, no one else will do it for you. Discipline today allows you to have the future you want.

Now it's time to review your budget. First, go through your budget and account for everything that is non-negotiable—things that you cannot cut out. Add all of those up. Compare that with your income. If that number alone is larger than your income, you will have to make drastic adjustments. You may have to find a different place to live or a different car to drive or make other significant life changes. You may have to refinance your debt. If you are in that place, you may need professional help. If you cannot find a way to get the non-negotiable monthly expenses lower than your current income, you may have to find a second job. There are many ways to restructure your spending. There is no hopeless case. For some of you, the answer may be getting help from a professional advisor.

If your non-negotiable monthly expenses are below your monthly income, then you can look at reducing the unnecessary items. The first time you review your budget, cut out all the "extras." Cut out the "luxury items." Things like cable TV or internet access or magazine subscriptions or cell phones should be considered luxuries while you are trying to get out of debt.

"But what am I going to do for fun or entertainment?" you might ask. How about starting your own business in order to make more money? How about developing a hobby into a money-making endeavor? How about going to the library to get more information? How about going to school to learn a new skill? How about learning to talk with your children or your spouse?

So many times we spend money unnecessarily, thinking we need things that are simply luxuries. There is nothing wrong with these things—or other things like them. But, when you are trying to escape the clutches of debt, luxuries are unnecessary and only make life more difficult for you. The money you spend on these things can be used to help you get out of debt more quickly.

If you thought that living on 70% of your income would cramp your style, you may be surprised to find that in order to pay off your debt you will have to live on 60% of your income or less. It may be painful in the short term, but in the long term it will pay great dividends for you.

Step 3: Focus on paying off the debt

Many people who do not understand financial principles make the mistake of not paying off debt when they get extra money. The focus of setting up a budget is to pay off the debt. Make it a priority to pay off the "bad debt" first. Things like credit-card debt must be the first to go.

Credit-card debt is the most expensive kind of debt you can have. Interest rates are ridiculously high—even if you have a so-called low-interest credit card. The monthly payments are designed to keep you paying for years. The actual amount you pay for the item, when you include the interest, is significantly more than the original purchase price.

The table below shows what credit cards cost us, if we carry debt. We used the average credit-card debt as of the writing of this book, which is $9,000 per household. The chart also shows how long it would take to pay off the debt and how much money you would have to pay each month in order to pay off the debt.

For Average Household Credit Card Balance of $9,000

Interest Rate On Card:	Initial Minimum Payment:	Number of Months to Pay Off Debt:	Amount of Interest Paid:
5.9%	**$225**	**199**	**$2,152.04**
13%	**$225**	**271**	**$6,703.31**
15%	**$225**	**304**	**$8,757.96**
18%	**$225**	**372**	**$13,115.36**
22%	**$225**	**539**	**$23,976.22**

Think about this with me. If you divide the number of months in the chart by 12, you can determine the number of years that it will take to pay off this $9,000 bill. In the best case, it will take you over *16 years* to pay off a $9,000 credit-card bill. In the worst case (where the interest rate is 22%), it will take *almost 45 years* to pay off this bill.

Remember, making a minimum payment only delays the creditors—it does not get rid of them. As people make these minimum payments, they face the constant prospect of missing a payment and having the creditors show up at their door.

Step 4: Have a vision for building wealth

As you pay off the debt, turn your attention to saving money and building wealth. Too many people make a crucial mistake as they pay off their debt. Instead of starting to save, they go back to their old ways and start to spend again. Having that extra money at the end of the month is a temptation to spend. They have been living under the discipline of the budget, so they justify loosening up a bit. Then, before they know it, because their old ways of thinking are so strong, they have lost the discipline they worked so hard to develop. Just when they can turn the corner and move into building wealth, they spend themselves back into debt.

Changing your thinking is so critical. Refuse to lose the discipline. Fight hard with your old thoughts. Start seeing what you can have with continued discipline.

To do that, set goals for the amount of money you want to save. Sit down and see what you can accumulate over time as you free up your money. Begin to build the mindset that you want your money to begin working for you rather than you working for money.

We begin putting our money to work for us when we begin to save. Start building a cash reserve. Set money aside so that when an unexpected expense arises, you have the cash to pay for it. Set money aside so you do not have to use credit cards to buy Christmas gifts. Set money aside so you do not have to use credit cards to pay for car repairs or maintenance.

Start seeing yourself paying cash for your next vacation. Start seeing yourself paying cash for your next car. Start seeing your home mortgage completely paid off. That may be a real stretch right now, but with continued discipline you can have it. It is not out of your reach. Other people, just like you, have done it. They learned the simple secret of spending less than they make and then managing the extra money well. You can do the same, if you are serious about getting out of debt.

IS BANKRUPTCY AN OPTION FOR A CHRISTIAN?

I want to share just a few thoughts with you on bankruptcy. The number of people who are spending themselves out of control and then filing bankruptcy is skyrocketing. In 2003, nearly 1.6 million Americans filed for bankruptcy.

Too many people think that filing bankruptcy is the solution for their money problems. Can I tell you something? Bankruptcy is not the solution. Filing bankruptcy does not change the way you think. Yes, it may relieve the financial pressure you face, but it does not change the real root of the problem, which is the way you manage money.

The world sees bankruptcy as a way out of financial difficulties. And because the legal system has made it relatively easy, Christians are beginning to accept it as the right thing to do. I want to challenge that thinking. I am not going to tell you what you can or cannot do, nor am I going to condemn you if you do file bankruptcy. I simply want to challenge your thinking. Bankruptcy is no guarantee that you will stay out of debt. If you do not put these common-sense ideas that we have discussed to work in your life, you will find yourself in the same financial difficulty after bankruptcy as you were before. Don't settle for the easy way out. Do the hard work to change the way you think about your finances. That is the only way to ensure that you will stay out of financial trouble.

IS BORROWING RIGHT FOR A CHRISTIAN?

I can summarize this whole book by saying that the only sure way to keep the creditors from coming to your home is to spend less than you make each month. When we do that, we will always have the money we need. We may not be able to fulfill our every whim and buy everything we want the first time we want it. But the simple philosophy of "I will spend less than what I make" will keep us from facing the financial pressure that so many are experiencing today.

Some may ask, "Does that mean that I should never borrow money?" A lot of current teaching in the Body of Christ says we are not supposed to borrow at all. I agree that being too far in debt is not good. But I also believe that there is a right time to borrow. Let's look at this in a bit more detail.

When we borrow because we want something now, we are borrowing for the wrong reason. That is simply a lack of discipline. Borrowing for something we want today, when we could save and pay cash for it in the future, is a poor choice.

If we borrow in order to have fun, we are making poor choices. If we borrow money to go on an expensive vacation, we are making a poor decision. Buying things with credit cards just because we want them now is not a wise move. Buying expensive cars, boats, and other recreational vehicles because we want to look good or drive the latest toy is not wise. Borrowing money to buy furniture, or borrowing money for things that will perish with use, is not wise. All of these are examples of what I will call "bad debt."

Why do I refer to them like that? All of these things decrease in value with use. When we borrow to buy things that will only decrease in value, we are making a foolish decision. These things can bring no additional value into our lives. In fact, most of them cause us to spend even more money.

However, when we borrow money to purchase something that increases with value, it may be a wise decision. For instance, borrowing money to buy a home is a wise decision when you compare it to renting. But we must be wise when we buy the house. Too many people buy too much house—just so they can impress someone else. Buy what you need, but don't buy so much that you become "house poor" —meaning that so much of your money is being spent on covering expenses for your home that you have nothing left to live on. That is a foolish home purchase.

Don't fall for a lot of the thinking in the financial world today when it comes to buying a home. The banks or the mortgage brokers will tell you that you can afford more of a home that you really can. Don't ever buy a home at the limit of your borrowing potential. Buy less than the limit of your potential. Build equity in your home over time. Then use that equity to make another wise home purchase in the future. That way you will always be moving ahead financially.

I also generally consider borrowing to start a business a wise type of borrowing. Now not every business opportunity deserves the risk that borrowing brings, but some do. When you have the opportunity to get into a business that has the potential to make money if you work hard, then that type of borrowing makes sense. You are borrowing to acquire an asset. An asset is something that has the power to make money for you.

Do you remember what Elisha told the widow woman in helping her get out of debt? He told her to borrow to get the assets she needed to turn her situation around. She had something in her home that had the ability to create wealth—the oil in the cruse. But she did not have the assets to make the oil produce for her. She had to borrow to get the assets she needed to start her business. If you look at most successful business people, you will discover that they had to borrow money to start a business.

Look at this profile of a successful businessman.

THEODORE WAITT, CEO & FOUNDER
GATEWAY COMPUTERS

- Born in Sioux City, Iowa
- Son of a fourth generation Iowa cattle farmer
- In 1985, got a $10,000 loan from his grandmother
- Co-founded Gateway computers at his family's Iowa farm
- In 2002, the revenue of Gateway Computers was ***$4.2 BILLION***
- Gateway has approximately 1,900 employees

The purchase of the asset will help you start a business and eventually will help you pay off the loan. That type of borrowing is wise at the right time and for the right opportunity.

Let's manage our finances with common sense. Then the creditors will never come to our home.

COMMON SENSE IDEAS

1. Money management is not that difficult.
2. God gives instructions to help each person solve their own problems, not just escape them.
3. Spending all that is made, even though a person makes a lot of money, doesn't make the person rich.
4. Wealth and income are not the same. Income is what you earn. Wealth is what you are worth.
5. Wealth comes as a result of spending less than what is made and wisely investing the difference.
6. "Maintenance-mode living" means spending everything earned.
7. "Maintenance-mode living" means going into debt for just one unexpected expense.
8. "Maintenance-mode living" is a doorway to mounting debt.
9. Individual discipline in spending leads to financial freedom.
10. Discipline in spending is not denial; it is only delay.
11. Finding out how much you owe is the first step in getting out of debt.
12. Create a vision for building wealth, not just for getting out of debt.

BUILD
A VISION FOR
MAKING MONEY
WORK FOR
YOU RATHER
THAN ALWAYS
WORKING
FOR MONEY.

Chapter 7

Build a Vision of Wealth

COMMON SENSE POINT 4:

***We must learn to save and invest wisely*—we can learn to make money work for us rather than working for money all of our lives.**

2 Kings 4:6-7 states:

"[6]Now it came to pass, when the vessels were full, that she said to her son, 'Bring me another vessel.'

*And he said to her, 'There is not another vessel.' So the oil ceased. [7]Then she came and told the man of God. And he said, '**Go, sell the oil and pay your debt**; and you and your sons **live on the rest**.'"*

In the previous chapter, I discussed some practical ideas about paying off debt to begin saving for the future. I want to expand a bit more on these thoughts—to challenge you to think about ways to start making money work for you, rather than spending your whole life working for money.

Too many people work for money, rather than making money work for them. They get up five mornings a week and go to a job they do not like. They spend eight or more hours each day working to earn enough money to do the things they really enjoy doing. Because they haven't had fun all week, they spend all the money they earn. That forces them to return to the job they do not like and do something they hate all of the next week, so they can spend all they earn doing what they want to do the next weekend. What a trap! This is what I mean when I say too many people are working for money, rather than making money work for them.

I have news for you. That is not God's plan for any of us. God never planned for any of us to work on a job we hate or to spend all the money we earn. This going-nowhere-fast-cycle-of-life is not God's plan for us. His plan is for money to be a servant to us, while we serve God. Matthew 6:24 states:

> *"24 No one can serve two masters; for either he will hate the one and love the other, or else he will be loyal to the one and despise the other. You cannot serve God and mammon."*

Any time we are working just to earn money, we are serving money, rather than serving God. And when we continue going to work just to earn money, and we spend all the resources earned from the job we hate, we become more and more of a servant to money.

God wants us to learn how to make money work for us, rather than having us work for money. That can happen when we learn to invest wisely.

CONSTANT INVESTING ACCUMULATES WEALTH FOR THE FUTURE!

Wealth is what you accumulate by saving and investing.

Galatians 6:7 in the Phillips Translation states: *"Don't be under any illusion: you cannot make a fool of God! A man's harvest in life will depend entirely on what he sows."*

This is a strong statement by the Apostle Paul. Notice that he says our harvest in life depends entirely on what we sow. I believe our investing is a form of sowing. That means we cannot spend all of our income. We must take a portion of it and place it into some sort of good investment.

You may be saying right now, "I cannot afford to invest money because I am so far behind in my bills." That may be so, but you cannot afford not to invest, because accumulating wealth depends on making wise investments. And if you have lived your whole life in debt, you need to start building a vision for a different type of lifestyle—a lifestyle where money works for you, rather than you always working for money. Each of us can have it.

It takes discipline to save money and to invest it, but living that way pays great dividends. One of the men in my church started saving by setting aside his income-tax return *every year* he got one. After a few years, he had enough money for a down payment on a home that he bought as a rental property. After he bought the house, he fixed it up and began renting it. That home then became a moneymaker for him.

How did he do it? By just being disciplined and having a vision. With both discipline and vision working in his life, he saved enough to buy an asset that began paying him.

But he didn't stop there. He kept saving his income-tax returns and was able to buy another home. He also fixed that up and began renting it. Today he owns numerous properties, and they are all making money for him. It all started with the simple step of disciplining himself to save his income-tax return and having a vision for making money work for him, rather than always having to work for money.

THE FUTURE EVENTUALLY COMES

When we're young, it's easy to think that our incomes will always be increasing and that we'll have plenty of time to save in the future. The truth is, the best time to save is when you are young. The earlier you begin to save, the longer your money has to work for you.

Developing the discipline to save is easier to do early in life, rather than later. And when you begin to save and invest earlier, your money has a longer time to work for you.

Let me show you the power of saving earlier in life. Here is an example for you to think about.

- **Individual A** is self-disciplined at age 22 and saves $3,000 a year, investing at the beginning of the year in a tax-deferred investment (such as an IRA) at a rate of return of 10% per year. Then, Individual A stops investing at age 32, and lets his/her money work.

- **Individual B** decides to "live a little" with money before starting to save—then, waits until age 32 to begin saving $3,000 a year until age 62.

Who do you think has more money when he is 62? Look at the chart on the following page for the answer….you might be surprised!

The Value of Saving Earlier Rather than Later in Life

Individual A			Individual B		
Age	Annual Savings	Accumulation at End of Year	Age	Annual Savings	Accumulation at End of Year
22	$3,000	$3,300	22	0	
23	$3,000	$6,930	23	0	
24	$3,000	$10,923	24	0	
25	$3,000	$15,316	25	0	
26	$3,000	$20,147	26	0	
27	$3,000	$25,462	27	0	
28	$3,000	$31,309	28	0	
29	$3,000	$37,740	29	0	
30	$3,000	$44,814	30	0	
31	$3,000	$52,595	31	0	
32	0	$57,855	32	$3,000	$3,300
33	0	$63,640	33	$3,000	$6,930
34	0	$70,004	34	$3,000	$10,923
35	0	$77,005	35	$3,000	$15,316
36	0	$84,706	36	$3,000	$20,147
37	0	$93,176	37	$3,000	$25,462
38	0	$102,494	38	$3,000	$31,309
39	0	$112,743	39	$3,000	$37,740
40	0	$124,018	40	$3,000	$44,814
41	0	$136,420	41	$3,000	$52,595
42	0	$150,062	42	$3,000	$61,155
43	0	$165,068	43	$3,000	$70,570
44	0	$181,575	44	$3,000	$80,927
45	0	$199,733	45	$3,000	$92,320
46	0	$219,706	46	$3,000	$104,852
47	0	$241,677	47	$3,000	$118,638
48	0	$265,844	48	$3,000	$133,802
49	0	$292,429	49	$3,000	$150,482
50	0	$321,672	50	$3,000	$168,830
51	0	$353,839	51	$3,000	$189,013
52	0	$389,223	52	$3,000	$211,215
53	0	$428,146	53	$3,000	$235,636
54	0	$470,960	54	$3,000	$262,500
55	0	$518,056	55	$3,000	$292,050
56	0	$569,862	56	$3,000	$324,555
57	0	$626,849	57	$3,000	$360,311
58	0	$689,533	58	$3,000	$399,642
59	0	$758,487	59	$3,000	$442,906
60	0	$834,336	60	$3,000	$490,497
61	0	$917,769	61	$3,000	$542,847
62	0	**$1,009,546**	62	$3,000	**$600,431**

Total Contributions: $30,000
Total Accumulation: $1,009,546

Total Contributions: $93,000
Total Accumulation: $600,431

See what I mean? Starting to save and invest earlier makes so much difference. The difference is amazing to me! Individual A pays the price to save $3,000 a year early in his life…and then does not save any more after that. Individual B does not pay the price to discipline himself to save early, so Individual B has to save *$63,000 more* than Individual A only to *have less money* at age 62 than Individual A. That just amazes me! Can you imagine *how much more money* Individual A would have had than Individual B if he would have kept saving $3,000 a year until he was 62? The difference would have been staggering!

Let's learn the value of saving earlier! Young people, please listen to me! Develop the discipline to save early! It will pay you well in the long run!

Now, some of you reading this book may have missed the opportunity to save when you were young. Please do not throw up your hands and give up. It is always better to save—no matter how old you are! Start now and save something. You will feel better now…and it will pay off for you later!

I gave you a formula earlier that I said would keep you from ever having financial difficulties. The formula was pretty straightforward. I encouraged you to pay your tithe (the first ten percent of your income). Then pay yourself (which means you save the next 20% of your income). Then you live on what is left (the remaining 70% of your income). I believe with that formula you will never face financial difficulties.

Living by that formula means you will put God first, save for the future, and manage your expenses. But now what should you be doing with the 20% you save?

Start with a savings account. Build up your cash reserves so that you always have a cushion for unexpected expenses. It is common sense that you should make it your goal to have at least six months' worth of income saved. That way, if for some reason your income was interrupted for a period of time, it would not have such a serious impact.

That is really the principle that Joseph used for Egypt. In the seven years of abundance, he saved 20% of the grain. Then when the seven years of famine came, he had more than enough grain in storage to feed the people. We can learn from that.

Once we have those cash reserves built up, we can focus on buying assets. An asset is anything that will generate money for us. Real estate is an asset. Buying a second home and renting it is an asset that makes money. Buying land and leasing it is an asset that makes money. Stocks and bonds and mutual funds are assets that, over time, have the potential to make money. Buying a company is an asset that will make money.

I mention these things just so you will understand what investing really is. Investing today will provide for a better future tomorrow. Of course, you could spend the 20% that I suggest you save, but that simply means you are mortgaging your future for a present need.

Let's get wise and start making our money work for us.

LEAVING AN INHERITANCE FOR YOUR FAMILY

As we close this common-sense approach to keeping the creditors from coming to your home, I want to talk about the financial responsibility we have to our families. I believe in leaving a legacy. Finances are one part of a legacy that we can and should leave for our families.

I believe it is our responsibility to leave an inheritance for our children. Too many of us, who are parents, are so shortsighted when it comes to our children. We think: "I gave my children life. I work hard to take care of them. I have sent them to college, and now that they are out of school, they are on their own." This is not biblical thinking. Now I do not believe that we are to support irresponsible adult children. On the other hand, we cannot live selfishly. We are required by God to provide not only for ourselves, but for our children and for their children. I am a firm believer that we should build, live, and leave a legacy for our children.

Let's talk about our responsibilities to our families for a bit. First, I believe we should have our affairs in order. One of the key things we need is a will. Whether you are single or married, you need a will. Why should you leave anyone with the responsibility of trying to figure out what to do with your assets after you die? A will can spell that out. A will can answer all those questions.

Second, each family should have some sort of life insurance. Whoever is the breadwinner for a family should have life insurance. If a man is the breadwinner for the family, the life insurance policy should be on him. If the wife makes more money, the policy should be on the wife. Use life insurance to protect the family from a sudden loss in income. It is never easy to lose a loved one. There are so many emotional challenges at that time. Why leave those who survive with the additional burden of trying to make ends meet? Life insurance allows a family to make a smoother transition after a death. It is one of the easiest things for a family to do, but I see so few people doing it.

Third, what about your home? Do you have enough insurance on your home? Now, I am not trying to be an insurance salesperson here, but I am being practical. Have enough insurance on your home to replace it and all your personal belongings, if something unforeseen should happen. None of us ever expects a fire or a flood, but those things do happen. Insurance shields you from those things. Again, it is easy to do and is relatively inexpensive in relation to the cost of losing a home.

When you get these things in place, make sure the people who need to know are aware of where things are. Husbands, make sure your wives know where all the important papers are. Make sure she understands where your money is. Make sure she knows your insurance agent. Make sure she knows where the will is and who to call about it. Don't leave her in the dark. Women need to feel secure, and this is one of the most important ways to make sure she feels secure.

COMMON SENSE NUGGETS

1. Build a vision for making money work for you, rather than always working for money.

2. Wealth is accumulated by saving and investing, rather than by spending all that is earned.

3. Saving for the future absolutely requires discipline.

4. Create a vision for building wealth, not just getting out of debt.

5. Use money saved to buy assets—not just spend it on pleasure.

6. It is wiser to save *less* earlier than to save *more* later.

7. Use insurance to protect your assets.

8. Responsible Christians should leave a financial legacy for their family; an inheritance should be left for our children.

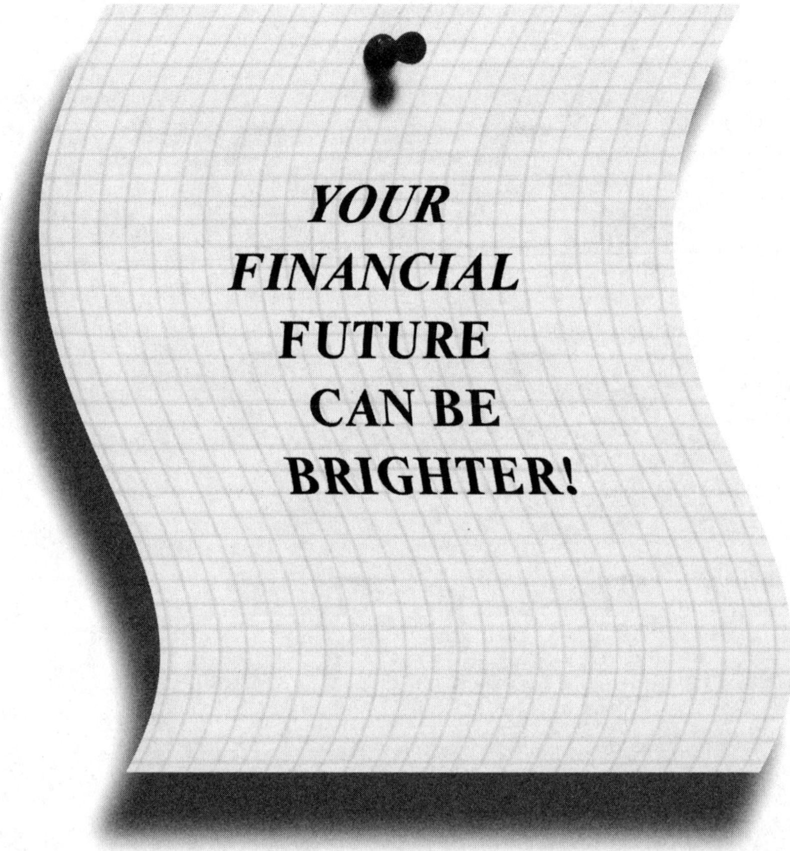
YOUR
FINANCIAL
FUTURE
CAN BE
BRIGHTER!

Conclusion

Everything I shared with you is designed to help you reap the benefits of a common-sense approach to managing your resources. I trust you were open and receptive to this. I know it is hard when you are in financial difficulties for anyone to tell you what to do. But, as a pastor, I love God's people too much to give them a myth about finances. It is my prayer that this book opened your eyes to common-sense methods to address financial issues.

I believe your financial future will be brighter because of your willingness to make the changes necessary to get out of debt. Just like the widow woman in 2 Kings 4 heard and obeyed the instructions from the man of God that turned her whole financial situation around and kept the creditors from taking away what was in her home, I believe the same can happen to you with this common-sense approach.

About the Author

Randy Morrison was born into poverty on the island of Trinidad in the West Indies in 1952. His unwed, 16-year-old mother dedicated her life to providing ways for her son to grow and prosper. Even as a child, the desire of Randy's heart was to find a better life for his mother and others. While a teenager, Randy's mother left him in Trinidad so she could seek better opportunities for them in the United States. Then, at the age of 19, Randy left Trinidad for the first time to reunite with his mother who had found employment in Minneapolis, Minnesota.

On November 7, 1971, Randy Morrison dedicated his life to Jesus Christ following a church service in the metropolitan Minneapolis area. This was the start of his dynamic, faith-filled journey. Responding to the vision revealed by God in his heart, Randy started Speak the Word Church on May 6, 1977, with only six people attending. Today, Randy's talents and gifts as a visionary leader are well known. Speak the Word Church International in Golden Valley, Minnesota, is a growing, non-denominational, interracial and international ministry dedicated to helping people discover and fulfill their God-given purpose through the gospel of the Kingdom of God. Hundreds of people attend services weekly at Speak the Word Church International.

Randy's common-sense approach to life inspires thousands. His international television broadcast—Common Sense Approach (www.commonsenseapproach.org)—is now seen in more than 150 countries worldwide. His focus and commitment to follow God's calling on his life more than 32 years ago is impacting lives throughout the world today. His common-sense message spans the world with the gospel of the Kingdom of God.

Randy is a sought-after speaker nationally and internationally. He is a living testimony to the truth that all things are possible with God. Application of Randy's common-sense approach is designed to help people live life by design and not from crisis to crisis.